Praise for the first edition

One Choice at a Time

A Practical Guide to Well-Being

"One Choice at a Time: A Practical Guide to Well-Being offers exceptional expert, compassionate and concrete guidance to psychological wellness. Readers are in for a treat!" ~Allison Reeves, MA, RCC

"This profoundly useful treasure chest of practices beautifully supports the life journey of anyone who hopes to live with greater ease and stillness. Counsellors, therapists and community practitioners will be inspired to weave many of these ideas into their good work with people." ~Yvonne Haist, MEd, RCC, Somatic Trauma Work Psychotherapist, Assistant Teaching Professor, University of Victoria

"Being able to do what matters most in life is for most people easier said than done. But with Susan Farling's new book, *One Choice at a Time: A Practical Guide to Well-Being*, almost anyone can learn how to achieve what matters most. Combining compelling rationale with simple, practical exercises, this book will not only provide the reader with confidence as to what to do, but also provide the techniques as to how to go about engaging in what matters most. Although everything in this book can be accomplished alone, I'd recommend buying two copies. Give one to a friend, and work on the ideas and activities together. Transformation is all the sweeter when someone else in your life can acknowledge, support, and cheer your journey." ~Rey Carr, Ph.D., CEO, Peer Resources

"I found the writing in *One Choice at a Time: A Practical Guide to Well-Being* to be clear and effective with easy-to-follow instructions on how to begin that personal journey when we are looking for clarity, purpose and direction either in our own lives or when we are helping our clients do the same. I wish there had been a book like this one when I was beginning my studies on becoming a counsellor. I highly recommend this book." ~Jocelyn Harris, MA, RCC

"I just sent a copy of *One Choice at a Time* to a relative. I think the book has invaluable wisdom - it can help build and strengthen the skills that help people navigate life's complex challenges." ~Anke van Leeuwen, RMT, Lay Counsellor

"Susan Farling, a master therapist, has created an opus that will serve as a gift to clients and to counsellors alike. This pithy volume contains gems of wisdom gleaned over Susan's career span and is informed by her experience with both western and eastern healing modalities. A book to return to again and again." ~Angela Burns, MA, RCC

"I want one for each of my kids!" ~Margaret Hantiuk, artist, editor, mother of adult children

"One Choice at a Time: A Practical Guide to Well-Being is full of both knowledge and practical wisdom that Ms. Farling has collected from decades of counselling experience, refined with hundreds of clients in practice. It contains many realistic and believable case examples that regular people can relate to.

But the real wealth of this book lies in its many clearly explained and practical exercises. These practices, pursued with kindness, willingness, interest, and patience guide the reader toward life improvements such as calmness, clarity in goals, compassion for self and others, self-worth, inner security, and gratitude.

Therapists too can benefit from this book both for personal use, and for the exercises which are explained step-by-step and with rich examples of how they can be applied in therapy practice. Depending on how far the reader takes these examples from *One Choice at a Time* into her or his own life, they will at a minimum learn something useful. If they take them seriously, they will emerge well equipped with practical tools for personal transformation." ~Brian Grady, Ph.D. Registered Psychologist

"I think your goals of having it be a self-help book as well as a resource for clinicians is well met." ~Ann Deatherage, retired nurse and clinical counsellor

Praise for the second edition

ONE CHOICE AT A TIME

A Practical Guide to Peace of Mind and Well-Being

"Susan Farling's years of experience working closely with people as a therapist and coach permeates the book — the frank and gentle tone, the way she stays with you to guide you through each exercise, the depth of the exercises broken down into practical small steps. In each exercise I felt Farling was holding my hand the whole way through — she consistently offers alternatives: what to do if answering this question is too difficult, what to do if your mind is blank, what to do if you are overwhelmed.

Susan teaches deep life skills and then weaves them throughout the book so that by the end of the book the skills of grounding and resourcing are second nature. This is a truly life changing book. This book can save your life! A grounded, practical, straight forward book that will nourish your heart and soul.

I had done some of these exercises before but Susan's examples and prompts were so authentic and presented with such clarity that they promoted a whole different kind of engagement for me. I'm grateful to have the opportunity to read this book. This is the medicine the world needs right now". ~Suiko Betsy McCall, Founder & Abbess, Art Monastery, Painter & Social Sculptor

One Choice at a Time invites readers to discover their own path to peace of mind and well-being. Susan's detailed instructions, specific activities and thought provoking questions ensure that this guidebook is accessible to all. This is a manual for life that can be read many times with relevance for different stages of life. As Susan so eloquently reminds us: "You can make choices based on your intention to support your well-being - choice by choice, breath by breath." ~Marjorie Warkentin, Author, Life Path Mentor and Speaker

"Anyone seeking insight into the purpose and direction of their life's journey will find helpful mind and body exercises inside *One Choice at a Time*. I believe the practises offered will be beneficial to anyone looking to live consciously, with gratitude and a desire to live a more purposeful life." ~Carol Thornton, retiree, devoted caregiver, mother, grandmother

"This sensitive and compassionate book is a guide to inner contentment and comfort with who you are. Susan shares her years of experience through story telling and gentle exercises that takes the reader on a journey that will open your heart to joy. I just love this book." ~Sandra Micheals, retiree and dedicated volunteer

ONE CHOICE AT A TIME

A Practical Guide

to Peace of Mind and Well-Being

Susan Farling, MA

Germaine Publishing

Victoria BC, Canada

DEDICATION

For Alysha, I love you, I celebrate you,

and I treasure our chats.

For my clients, thank you.

I've been blessed by your trust.

For you reading, this book is for you.

May it serve you well.

DISCLAIMER

The information in this book is not intended as a substitute for face-to-face psychotherapy or counseling or medical attention; nor is it intended to be a substitute for or against the advice of attending psychotherapists, psychologists, psychiatrists or medical doctors. While the practices and exercises in this book may be useful, neither the author nor Germaine Publishing intends to present specific psychological, emotional or medical advice.

The people, stories and events described in *ONE CHOICE AT A TIME A Practical Guide to Peace of Mind and Well-Being* were created from an amalgamation of characteristics that reflect client reality, recurring themes, and real-life experiences. All names and identifying details of clients described in this book have been thoroughly and carefully changed to protect their privacy and anonymity. Any similarity to any actual person or situation is completely coincidental and is indicative of the universality of the concerns discussed here.

Although the author and publisher have made every effort to ensure that the information in this book was correct at press time, including correct acknowledgements and accurate internet addresses, the author and Germaine Publishing do not assume and hereby disclaim any liability to any party for any changes after publication, or any loss, damage, or disruption caused by errors or omissions, whether such errors or omissions result from negligence, accident, or any other cause. Any errors or omissions will be gratefully acknowledged and corrected in subsequent volumes of this book.

For your free

ONE CHOICE AT A TIME

Full Body Relaxation Audio

go to

susanfarling.com/free-gift-audio-full-body-relaxation-lp/

CONTENTS

PREFACE

The changes made in the second edition of this book are as follows: 1) a change of title from *One Choice at a Time: A Practical Guide to Well-Being* to *One Choice at a Time: A Practical Guide to Peace of Mind and Well-Being* 2) change of cover 3) removal of the QR code explanation and QR codes 4) removal of links in the body to videos and audios (to be replaced by an audiobook) 5) inclusion of a link to a relaxation audio in front and back matter 6) minor edits and brief additions, none of which alter the substance of the book 7) use of the Canadian spelling 'counsellor' (81% to 19% preference in Canada), rather than 'counselor' which is used in the United States (98% to 2% preference).

First and second edition endorsements of the book are included. Regretfully, the ever kind and inclusive Dr. Rey Carr died in 2019.

INTRODUCTION

"Yesterday's fog dissolves in the luminous present."
~SF

The Yellow Pages

Jen was back in my office for a tune up after two years of travel. She'd just settled into her chair and was rummaging through her battered leather bag, first pulling out a lime green scarf, then notebooks, a water bottle, her glasses case and now a crumpled square of lined yellow paper which she unfolded with a flourish. "See! I've kept it with me all this time!" It was a piece of foolscap covered with my scrawled writing—homework suggestions from her last counselling session with me.

For years I've jotted suggestions for homework on yellow foolscap at the end of a session. Clients have told me that they put their homework on their fridges, tape it to their mirrors, keep it in their back pockets, but never had a yellow page come back after a two-year stint in Southeast Asia!

Jen told me that she'd used the practices I'd written on that foolscap as ways to stay healthy as she traveled. She said that doing regular physical and mental exercises helped her stay grounded and present in unfamiliar surroundings.

The homework suggestions I'd given Jen included several simple yet powerful practices that I've learned over a lifetime. I've used them throughout the years to support my own and hundreds of clients' peace of mind and well-being. I've witnessed their benefits and know from the inside out the transformational opportunities they offer.

Twenty-seven years after opening my private practice, I wrote *One Choice at a Time: A Practical Guide to Well-Being* based on the foundational bodymind practices I taught and continue to teach and use. I included examples of how clients (described here as composites of real people, with identities carefully and thoroughly concealed) have incorporated these practices into their daily lives.

Five years later, I've named the second edition of this book *ONE CHOICE AT A TIME: A Practical Guide to Peace of Mind and Well-Being*, as achieving and maintaining peace of mind is especially challenging for many of us in the face of compounding global crises and is one of the main outcomes of practicing the exercises in this book.

My Story

I was born and raised in an isolated coastal village surrounded by rainforest. I was an only child and a dreamer. I loved the trees, the rain, the inlet waters, the nearby lake. At home, I'd get lost in the beauty of soap bubbles when I was expected to be efficiently doing dishes. I often heard "Use your head!" I found this very confusing as I didn't know what to do differently. As I grew, I was told too often that I didn't think what I thought, mean what I said, feel what I felt, or want what I wanted. In my tense family home, I learned to doubt myself, to feel guilty and anxious.

I left home at seventeen, eager to adventure off to the big city and university. An undergraduate degree in drawing and painting began an ongoing love of and respect for the creative process. When my first marriage ended after five years, I was unprepared for my emotional turmoil and the depression that followed. It gradually dawned on me that while I'd left home physically, what I'd learned as a child had traveled with me. I began to look for meaningful guidance on how to live a life that made sense to me. I explored the practical wisdom of the East and West; traveled and worked a hodgepodge of jobs. I meditated, practiced yoga, and entered therapy. I was determined to transform myself from the inside out and eventually help others do the same.

By the time I was thirty, curiosity about what made some people more resilient than others whetted my appetite for more formal education. This led me to a decade-long career as a registered nurse working mainly in acute care psychiatry. I gravitated towards using a client-centered approach with patients—an approach for which there was little institutional support at that time. Wanting to step aside from the prescriptive medical model, I went back to university and obtained a graduate degree in counselling psychology. While in that program I expanded my longstanding interest in Eastern philosophy. I took a post-graduate internship in psychotherapy and then followed up with several years of bodymind studies. As I did this my appreciation for the wisdom of the bodymind grew and continues to do so to this day.

When my only child was two and I was forty-three, I opened my private practice in counselling and psychotherapy. For the first time in my working life, I felt that I could meaningfully use myself and my experiences to support my clients. In my office, along with the skills I'd learned during my formal education, I began to offer the mindful, body-oriented practices that had supported my own profound shifts and that I continue to use to maintain my peace of mind and well-being.

Who is this book for?

ONE CHOICE AT A TIME will be a resource for people who've not done any personal inner work and who want to make positive life changes. It'll be useful for readers who may have encountered an upsetting circumstance or challenging life transition and who want how-to guidance for staying steady during those times. It could be a vague sense of uneasiness about their lives that brings other readers to this book. Some may be fed up with repeating unproductive patterns that don't serve them and be ready to learn to support themselves from the inside out. Still others may simply want a refresher of familiar practices—a tune-up.

As well, a new counsellor, therapist, or coach can use this book as a resource if they want to incorporate clearly laid-out, basic bodymind exercises and techniques into their clinical practices.

A centuries-long western assumption has been that the mind and body are separate, and that the body is machine-like and at the service of the mind. I used the term bodymind in this book to indicate the now well-documented reality that the body and mind are in constant, reflective, complex communication. Reverend Suzuki Roshi addressed that relationship succinctly when he said "...our mind and body are both two and one." (Suzuki, Shunryu. *Zen Mind Beginner's Mind Transcripts, Lecture on Posture.* 1965).

Bodymind well-being includes physical awareness, health, and vitality; mental alertness and competency; engagement with and satisfaction in relationships; a sense of living with connection, meaning, and purpose; a capacity for experiencing pleasure, satisfaction, and awe; and a healthy dose of that intangible, delightful joie de vivre. (adapted from Huseyin, Naci & Ioannidis, John. *Evaluation of Wellness Determinants and Interventions by Citizen Scientists.* JAMA, 2015). Of course, there's more, and we'll touch on other aspects of bodymind well-being in the exercises in this book.

This book and these exercises are not a substitute for counselling or psychotherapy. If you're reading or listening to this book and are feeling distraught, desperate, or suicidal, please reach out for help—to a professional person, to a trusted friend, or to a family member.

Let's begin.

CHAPTER 1: BENEFICIAL ATITUDES

"One kind word can warm three winter months."
~Japanese Proverb

Welcome to *ONE CHOICE AT A TIME: A Practical Guide to Peace of Mind and Well-Being.* If you decide to engage wholeheartedly with the exercises in this book, they'll help you increase your self-awareness so that you can recognize and challenge undermining and limiting habits of thoughts, beliefs, and behaviors that keep you from feeling peaceful and confident in your choices. You'll learn proven ways of supporting your resourcefulness, resilience, and well-being. By the time you work your way through the exercises, you'll know how to support yourself through challenging times. You'll enjoy yourself more, relax more often and feel more energetic. You may even find yourself having unexpected bouts of happiness as you learn to live more fully in the present.

The following are some beneficial attitudes—meaning how you feel, think, and behave as well as your manner or posture—that will help you practice and integrate the skills introduced in *One Choice at a Time* with ease and confidence in the process.

Kindness

Getting to know your own thoughts and feelings can feel uncomfortable and even scary. Not everyone starts out as an eager explorer. Often it's a painful experience that provides the impetus to make changes. Some people are afraid of what they might find if they look, and so they turn to outward distractions. Others cringe at what they see or feel and ask, "How could I be so stupid?" I encourage you to practice kindness with yourself as you go through all the exercises.

Starting right now—kindness! Even if you were to close this book and never pick it up again, or stop listening to the audio, practice kindness.

Does this suggestion seem strange or impossible? Do this: ask yourself, whenever you're treating yourself less than kindly or even harshly, "How would I be talking to myself and treating myself if I were kind to myself right now?" If you don't know, think of someone you like or love and ask yourself, "How would I be speaking to my friend right now?" Then do that for yourself.

There are several exercises in this book that will help you develop inner kindness.

If you think this is self-indulgent, I invite you to practice the beneficial attitude of willingness.

Willingness

In counselling, people are often asked to adopt attitudes or behaviors that are unfamiliar to them. For example, a client talking about a current upset may be invited just to sit with what she's feeling and notice what's happening in her body—even though she may usually ignore her feelings and sensations. It may feel uncomfortable to consciously allow a sensation to emerge and to observe it moving through the body. It may require a leap of faith to continue. If this is true for you, practice for just a few breaths. Gradually build your tolerance for noticing your physical sensations. Because your mind and body are in a seamless loop of communication and influence, you'll get to know yourself much better by attending to yourself this way.

EXERCISE 1.1 Experience a Closed Versus an Open Attitude

Here's a simple exercise for you to physically experience the contrast between a closed attitude and a willing, interested one:

Step 1: Exaggerate Tension with a Closed Posture

- First, cross your arms and legs and hunch your shoulders. Look down and toward one of your shoulders and frown. That's a closed-off posture.

- Exaggerate any tension you may feel and hold the position for several breaths.

- Then shift and take a couple of relaxing, tension-releasing breaths.

Step 2: Release Tension for an Open Posture

- Next, to embody an attitude of willingness, raise your head and look forward, soften your gaze, allow your shoulders to relax and drop. Uncross your arms and legs. To add a feeling of expansiveness, breathe gently and deeply and open your arms in a welcoming, embracing gesture, palms up. Feel the difference?

If you find yourself feeling closed-off or skeptical about any of the exercises offered here, ask yourself to consider moving in the direction of willingness. Soften and open your physical posture. You'll notice a concurrent shift in your mental attitude. You'll get the most benefit from the *ONE CHOICE AT A TIME* exercises if you approach them with an open, curious, and willing attitude.

Here's an example of one of my clients demonstrating willingness in action:

Ted's Story

Ted, stocky, dark-haired, and muscular at thirty, thrived on the male camaraderie he found in coaching and playing soccer. He relished twice weekly social time with his "brothers." It hadn't occurred to him that Cheryl, his wife, who had recently given birth to their second daughter, deeply resented his absences or that she felt neglected and unseen by him. After all, he told me, he was home more than his own very traditional father had been, and babies weren't really his "thing." He was providing for his family and not, in his words, "screwing around." Cheryl, who'd recently come into an inheritance, gave Ted an ultimatum. Things between them had to change drastically. She wanted to see a lot more of him, or, now that she had the financial means to do so, she was prepared to leave with the children.

Ted told me that there was no way he would have come to counselling if it hadn't been for his shock and dismay over the potential loss of his family. He said that until then he'd felt scornful of men he thought were weak because they'd asked "some stranger" for help. Ted said he was committed to doing whatever he had to do to save his family. He was willing to meet with me in the unfamiliar counselling setting. He was willing to challenge some of his deeply held beliefs and long-standing behaviors.

Ted did his work and within six weeks he and Cheryl had started couples counselling.

Interest and Curiosity

Experiment with having an interested and curious researcher attitude toward yourself and your results. Be as matter-of-fact as you can. Don't make yourself right or wrong.

Practice the exercises as wholeheartedly as you are able and notice your thoughts, feelings, and behaviors. Especially notice with interest which of these move you in the direction of your goal of peace of mind and well-being and which do not. Also notice which thoughts, feelings, and behaviors that may be briefly enjoyable but don't support you in reaching your longer-term goals. For example, a judgmental, critical thought about a friend may feel righteously energizing for a moment but later leave you feeling uneasy and disconnected from that person. For many people, it's challenging to observe themselves without making comments such as "I'm never going to get this" or "This is too hard" or "I can't believe I'm such an idiot." Rather than making negative comments on what you notice, practice saying to yourself: "Isn't that interesting!"

Here's an example of a client using an interested and curious attitude to review her experience with doing homework:

Felicia's Story

In her first counselling session, Felicia told me that she used to love journal writing. She said it had helped her move into a deeply nourishing creative space. For the past several years she'd been so busy raising her two young girls, now twenty months and three years old, and bookkeeping for her husband's business, that she simply hadn't had time to write. She was feeling overwhelmed and as though she had lost her inner spark. At the end of our session, I asked Felicia if she would consider writing in her journal again. She thought this would be a good idea but was concerned about feeling even more overloaded and time challenged. Together we worked out a writing schedule that she thought would be doable.

At her next session, Felicia and I reviewed, with interest and curiosity, how that plan worked out. Did she write? *It turned out that she had, though not as often as she'd planned.* Given that she had written, how did she feel about that? *Felicia said that she felt relieved to have started writing but was trying to not feel disappointed with herself for not sticking with her initial plan. She was also annoyed that she'd let her writing skills get rusty.* Did writing move her in the direction of being more in touch with her creativity, which was one of her goals in coming to counselling? *Yes, Felicia smiled and said she was clear that writing in her journal had done that much.* Were there any internal blocks she could identify that got in the way of her writing? *Felicia identified, as a familiar internal block, feelings of guilt for wanting time away from her children.* What in her environment was supportive of her writing? *Felicia's two sisters were enthusiastically supportive of her taking time for herself and were ready and willing to schedule turns to look after their nieces.*

By developing a kind internal attitude and

asking questions about her new undertaking with matter-of-fact curiosity and interest, Felicia was developing the internal objectivity she needed to see how she was both supporting and undermining herself. By supporting herself to journal guilt-free, Felicia learned to support her peace of mind.

Trust

Children learn to trust themselves and others when they have at least one responsive and loving caregiver who meets their developmental needs. As they mature, well-nurtured children are likely to face life's challenges with resilience and to move in the world with confidence that baffles the less secure. As trustworthy adults themselves, they are caring and reliable, and follow through on their commitments. They're likely to be open to new experiences, trust their own perceptions, and assume the goodwill of others. They're perceptive in evaluating the people around them and discerning about when trust in others is warranted. They want the people in their lives to be trustworthy.

Here's an example of a client learning to trust his own wisdom

Bart's Story

Bart, a slender, intense man in his late sixties, came in saying that he felt stuck. Over the course of several sessions, he unearthed and challenged some of his limiting beliefs and assumptions. During his fourth session, I wrote what Bart said as he talked. By the end of the session, I had noted several of his ideas for his next action steps. When Bart asked, "Aren't you going to give me homework?" I handed him the page with the action steps he had decided were important. He read them and said, "Wow, that's fantastic! That's exactly what I need to do."

Bart was able to give his own words authority and value when he saw them written on the familiar yellow homework foolscap. He said that he felt energized, confident, and capable of following through with his plans, which he recognized were his own.

Many of you, like Bart, already know how you want to feel and what you need to do to get there. You may lack the confidence to trust your own wisdom or your ability to change, and may feel stuck, locked into old habits and familiar patterns. One way you'll build trust in yourself is to keep your commitments to yourself and gradually integrate what you learn by doing the exercises in *ONE CHOICE AT A TIME*. With this inner foundation, you'll develop new, productive, consciously chosen habits.

As you learn to trust in your inherent resourcefulness, resilience, and wisdom, your peace of mind will grow.

Patience

The creation of new, healthy habits requires repeated practice. Inner repetitions are the equivalent of doing a physical workout. You don't expect that one visit to the gym will give you, or help you maintain, a toned and fit body. It's the same with developing life-affirming internal attitudes. Periods of new peace, clarity, or increased energy are clues that your inner reps are working.

Acknowledge the moments, however fleeting, when you feel more the way you want to feel. Have patience and notice if you're tempted to discount such a moment because it didn't last.

Over time, given wholehearted practice of the exercises suggested in this book, these periods of grace will last longer and become your new norm. Like going to the gym, for internal work you need a plan for maintaining this new fitness. The practices you'll learn here will work to both kick-start new habits and serve as maintenance routines. They will work for you if you work with them and keep your focus on what you really want in your life!

An example of a client demonstrating patience:

Sandy's Story

Sandy, an athletic twenty-three-year-old, came to counselling because she wanted to feel more confident. She had the habit of calling herself "disgusting" when she glanced in the mirror. She believed that her harsh assessment of herself was "the truth."

Sandy had grown up in a family that placed a high value on women looking polished and manicured. Because Sandy degraded herself about her looks, one of her first homework suggestions was to name and challenge that self-negating habit. Sandy decided that 'mean girl' worked for her. When she caught herself saying, as she glanced in a mirror, "Ugh, you're disgusting." she decided to switch to saying energetically, "I wouldn't take that from anyone else and I won't take it from myself, either!" She followed up with, "Sorry self, that's my mean girl and I'm learning to treat myself with respect and caring." She learned to turn her attention away from her inner putdown and refocus with a cleansing and releasing breath. She then coached herself to say something kind or acknowledging to herself to counter and replace her inner mean girl insult.

Initially, it was hard for Sandy to find supportive things to say to herself, however, she was fueled by determination. She stuck with her new practice with patience for the need for repetition of new behavior and after several weeks started to enjoy finding alternative, believable, and kind things to say to herself. As she persevered, Sandy built up her new habit of self-care and self-respect and consequently supported her peace of mind. She re-connected with a humorous and playful side of herself that she remembered from her pre-adolescent days.

Sandy told me that she was not only feeling more relaxed about her physical appearance but was also feeling lighter and more confident in general.

"I don't even want to look like them." she

*laughed, referring to her sisters and her mother.
"I don't even like nail polish and perfume."*

Self-Responsibility

People come into my office saying that they want inner peace, clarity, more energy, and better relationships. They say they want less stress. What often emerges is that they really want another person to change in a way that seems so reasonable, so obvious, and then all would be well. A husband just needs to change an irritating habit; parents have only to finally acknowledge the pain they inflicted years ago; a boss ought to step up to the managerial plate and offer a raise. Then all would be well. Or perhaps it's the school, the house, the country that needs to change.

The good news (which may initially seem like bad news) is that the only person you have any real control over is yourself—your thoughts, your attitudes, your beliefs, your physical well-being, your emotional life, your behaviors—only yours.

We are all profoundly influenced by our families, our cultures, government policies, and the environment. We live in a rich soup of nuanced, often compelling interrelatedness. You can best serve yourself and the people around you, however, by embracing the stance that you are responsible for the life you are creating, moment by moment, breath by breath.

There are many examples of people who—by virtue of taking charge of their own inner lives with determination, vision, faith, and perseverance—have overcome what to others might have been daunting or crushing circumstances.

Please note: True assumption of self-responsibility does not encourage a blame-the-victim attitude. Nor does it excuse or deny the impact of others' abusive behavior. If you're in a violent or controlling relationship, please support yourself by getting meaningful help.

Here's an example of a man turning his impulse to blame into self-responsible behavior:

Richard's Story

> *Richard was going through a painful divorce. He felt deeply betrayed by his soon-to-be ex, Connie. He was bitter, blaming, and awash with feelings of humiliation. He wanted to hurt Connie as he believed she'd hurt him. Richard was adversarial when it came to splitting assets and contemptuous in their exchanges.*
>
> *In counselling, he became aware of his regret for the way he'd behaved toward Connie during their twelve-year marriage. Richard began to see points where he could have chosen to behave*

differently. A breakthrough came when he took responsibility for his part in the marriage breakdown. As he did this, Richard felt much less victimized by Connie and much more conscious of the negative impact his own current choices were having on his mental attitude and self-esteem.

Richard began to make choices based on his view of what was fair rather than on his urge for revenge and liked himself much more as a result.

Necessary Self-Care

Some people wonder if they have the right to attend to their own suffering when they think others have it so much worse.

Here is an example of one such client:

Leslie's Story

It was painfully obvious that Leslie, a young woman in her late teens, was uncomfortable coming in for counselling. She sat opposite me, perched on the edge of her seat, her head bowed, blond hair covering her face and asked hesitantly, "Do I have the right to take your time?"

Leslie had just described how she wasn't as grateful as she believed she should be in her relationships with friends and family. She said that she often felt resentful about small things that she thought shouldn't matter. She also described being painfully aware of how responsible she felt when anyone around her was unhappy, or out of sorts. She was feeling guilty, unhappy, and burdened, and she didn't believe that she had the right to feel any of that. Leslie said, "On the surface, everything is fine and so many people have it so much worse." I told her that her concerns were very worthy of both of our attention.

Like Leslie, you may live your life focused outwardly on activities or on the needs and wants of others. You may believe that to do otherwise is selfish. This belief can be reinforced by the grumbles of your companions when you change the status quo and say that, for example, you'll no longer be making lunches every day of the week. If your belief about selfishness or the disapproval of others, real or imagined, keeps you in line, resentment can creep in. Instead of judging your resentment, just notice it. It may be a clue that you're over-extended or that you would like the support and help that is being asked of you. It's time to consider your inner life and values and realign either your attitudes or your actions. Initially, this may seem inconvenient or unfair.

Reminding yourself that you are choosing to do the activities you resent (even if you don't feel as though you have options) is a good place to start.

Once Leslie learned to validate her own feelings, she started courageously experimenting with setting boundaries with her overbearing older sister, Haille. First Leslie simply noticed situations where she felt resentful, without saying anything out loud. She thought about what she might say and mentally rehearsed this by visualizing herself speaking up. In the past, Leslie had only said "no" to Haille if she was exhausted or angry. She was relieved to learn that she could set clear boundaries calmly, respectfully, even lovingly, and for many reasons. Very soon she was impatient with simply observing her choice points and felt confident enough to be direct and clear. Leslie risked telling Haille "I'm not available today" rather than a lukewarm "Alright, I'll do it."

Leslie said that she was amazed at how well it

had gone and how energized she felt. She said that she felt hopeful about developing a new, more equal relationship with her sister.

In her last session, Leslie commented that counselling had been "worth it."

If you're reading this book because something in your life isn't working for you, I invite you to read on.

Practice the exercises and surprise yourself with your new perspective, clarity, peace of mind, and expanded sense of what is possible in your life.

Chapter 2: Relaxed Anticipation

"Tension is who you think you should be. Relaxation is who you are." *~Chinese Proverb*

Have you ever been right in the middle of a Big Worry only to have a well-meaning colleague or friend say, "Ahh, don't worry about it—re-laaax." Easier said than done and not very helpful advice in that context! All those concerns that bring people into counselling, and that brought you to read or listen to this book create tensions in our bodyminds that we unwittingly bind in place and reinforce with our repetitive worries and often righteous mullings. Considered at a time when we can actually hear it, however, the advice to relax is brilliant.

Relaxation is one of the most healing, rejuvenating, and kind things we can offer ourselves.

Without the opportunity to deeply and regularly relax, the buildup of tension that we carry can lead to a chronically elevated stress response, and eventually to bodymind systems breakdown and disease. And how much more enjoyable it is to embark on any journey with relaxed anticipation rather than frenzied anxiety, or to participate in an activity in a state of relaxed alertness rather than feeling on guard, exhausted, or dull.

Many harried people hear this and say, "I understand the benefits, I just don't have the time to relax. I have a job. I'm raising children. I'm a full-time university student. Exactly when did you think I could fit in relaxation?" It's a great question. I remember the year when I had a young child and a stressful part-time nursing job in acute care psychiatry. I'd recently completed a master's degree, purchased a house, and started my private practice. During all that business and my resultant exhaustion, I developed a severe chronic illness that I had to manage for years. Fortunately, I gradually found my way back to health. Since experiencing my own health crisis, I'm more alert to the potentially devastating outcome of chronic tension or exhaustion in myself and in my clients.

Regardless of how busy you are, it's imperative that you start integrating regular times of relaxation into your life.

There are a number of ways to do this. I'll suggest a few that will help you shift gears just enough to make a big difference.

The following is a Breath Focusing-Tension Releasing technique adapted from Western medicine's *The Relaxation Response* (Dr. Herbert Benson, 1975) and my years of experience with various meditative practices. It's a potentially very powerful relaxation technique that you can use to stay calm when waiting in a lineup or when you're faced with an upset co-worker, an aggressive or distracted driver, or a screaming child. With a relaxed bodymind, you can steady yourself, stay calm, and have access to your flexibility, creativity, and overall emotional intelligence even in a stressful situation.

This practice will be effective if you do it regularly. Don't leave it until the tough times. This is a skill you'll want to have in your back pocket so that it'll be ready for you when you need it.

EXERCISE 2.1 Breath Focusing-Tension Releasing Techniques (also called BFTR Techniques)

The Long Form

Before you start: If you feel anxious doing this or any exercise suggested in this book—please stop. Gradually open your eyes in three soft blinks. Bring yourself into the present by shifting your focus to the feel of your feet on the floor, your weight in the chair. Notice the texture of the furniture, the sounds you hear, the colours you see. Have a drink of tea or water. Stretch and move your body. There are effective short forms of this exercise described later in this chapter. It's important that the exercises in this book work for you.

While you're learning the following technique, make sure you have privacy, are well supported in a relaxed, alert posture, have both feet on the floor (or on a cushion if you are short), and have your spine straight.

Take at least twenty minutes to practice this exercise thoroughly without distraction. Give yourself the gift of your focused attention.

Read or listen to the instructions once completely, then go through the exercise one step at a time until you've mastered each step. After that, combine the three steps into the complete Long Form Breath Focusing-Tension Releasing technique.

To better focus, while you learn, do this with your eyes closed, if you are comfortable doing so. If you are not comfortable closing your eyes, soften and lower your gaze as you practice. Of course, when you are out and about, you'll keep your eyes open when you use this technique.

Notice your current level of tension or relaxation. Give yourself a number between one and ten, one being calm and peaceful and ten being agitated and upset: ______. When you finish the exercise, you'll be prompted to give yourself another number. Notice how it compares to the original. There are no right or wrong numbers. This suggestion is solely for you to have a way to check your bodymind response to this exercise.

Step 1: Anchor on Your Breath

- Shift your attention from your thoughts, or the sounds and activity around you, to the sensation of air moving in and out of your nostrils.

- Stay with that sensation. You'll notice that your mind wanders. That's okay and to be expected. Just calmly and patiently refocus your attention on your breath over and over.

- What does it feel like to have air coming in and out of your nostrils? Is one nostril more open than the other?

Don't try to change your breath in any way. You're just noticing what's there.

Do this for at least six breaths to practice gently but firmly refocusing your attention on the sensations of air in your nostrils, over and over, when your mind wanders. Practice patience.

- Now, as you inhale, begin to follow your breath with your attention as it enters and leaves your lungs.

- Notice the variations in expansions and contractions that happen in your chest, ribs and abdomen as you breathe in and out.

- Notice this for several breaths, and when your mind wanders, anchor your attention on the sensations of air going in and out of your nostrils.

- Then return to observing your fuller breath.

Step 2: Name Your Breaths

Silently name your breaths "Breathing in" on your inhalation and "Breathing out" on your exhalation.

- Keep your attention on your breath as you inhale fully through your nose, naturally, without straining. Imagine that your breath is flowing right down into your abdomen. Say silently to yourself, "Breathing in."

- As you exhale, either through your nose or through slightly pursed lips, without straining, say silently to yourself, "Breathing out." Make your exhalations longer than your inhalations.

Stay with this for at least six breaths for the purposes of this learning exercise.

- Again, you'll notice that your mind wanders. When you notice this, patiently re-anchor on your breath, on the sensations of air in your nostrils, for a breath or two, then go back to observing your fuller breath and saying silently to yourself, "Breathing in" on your inhalations and "Breathing out" on your exhalations.

Step 3: Let Go of Tension

- Maintaining your attention on your breath, say silently on your inhalation, "Breathing in." On your exhalation say silently, "Breathing out and releasing tension—letting go."

- As you exhale, allow your whole body to soften, even a little. Let your chair hold you up. Make sure your fingers and toes are soft, with no clenching, as you say on your exhalation, "Releasing tension, letting go."

- Imagine tension flowing out on your breath, through your pores, and out of your fingers and your toes.

Your imagination is powerful. Too often you use it to imagine scenarios that cause you to tense up. Here you have a constructive way to use your wonderful, creative imagination for your own benefit.

Stay with this practice of saying silently on your inhalation "Breathing in" and saying silently on your exhalation "Breathing out and releasing tension, letting go" for at least six breaths for the purpose of this learning exercise.

Remember to soften your fingers and toes on your exhalation.

To come out of the exercise, gradually open your eyes with three slow blinks.

Notice the level of tension or relaxation in your body and give it a number between one and ten. Again, one is calm, peaceful, and relaxed, and ten is agitated and upset: _______. How does this number compare to the number you gave yourself before you started the exercise? Remember, there is no right or wrong number. Use your attitude of interested curiosity when observing whether or not the BFTR exercise helped you move in the direction of more relaxation.

Following completion of this three-step practice, focus your attention in a positive direction. For example, you could:

- take a moment to have a glass of water.

- remind yourself what you appreciate about your life and the people around you.

- admire a plant or pet a cat. Listen to music. Dance.

- tell yourself, "This too will pass."

In doing the Long Form Breath Focusing-Tension Releasing technique, you're learning to use breath to create an internal pause so that you can shift from the tension of thoughtless reactivity into more expansive self-aware responsibility.

Our emotional reactions are caused by the meaning we assign an event, not the event itself. Take the example of the range of reactions people have to rain. Person A might look out, curse, and say, "What a lousy day. I hate the rain." while person B might anticipate getting out and about under an umbrella. Person C might be delighted to curl up with a good book and enjoy the sound of rain on the roof. Same event, different people, different responses.

When you are well-practiced in the Long Form Breath Focusing-Tension Releasing technique, you can use the abbreviated version described below. It's a potent and useful tool that you can use to sidestep internal reactivity long enough to engage your more thoughtful self.

Breath Focussing-Tension Releasing, The Short Form

Step 1: Notice Tension

- You notice you're starting to tense up. You identify that you're reacting to some internal trigger such as a judgmental, blaming thought, or an apparently external trigger, such as undone dishes.

- You remind yourself, "It's how I'm reacting that is causing my upset." Remember, it's not the rain that caused the different reactions in the example given earlier. It's what persons A, B, and C thought and felt about the rain. It's not the undone dishes causing your upset, it is the meaning you make about their being undone that is upsetting you. ("He never listens to me.")

- No matter how irritated you feel, or how justified you believe your reaction to be, or how compelling your thoughts are, shift your attention away from the apparent trigger and instead anchor on your breath, on the sensations of air in your nostrils for one inhalation/exhalation round.

Step 2: Name the Breaths

- On your next breath, say silently to yourself "Breathing in" on the inhalation through your nose and "Breathing out" on the exhalation.

Step 3: Release Tension, Come Present

- On your third breath, say silently to yourself "Breathing in" on your inhalation and "Breathing out and releasing tension, letting it go" on your exhalation.

- Soften your body as you exhale through your nostrils or slightly pursed lips. Make sure your fingers and toes are relaxed. Imagine tension streaming gently from your body. Feel your weight on the chair, your feet on the floor, the quality of the air on your skin. Notice any sounds around you. Doing this you come more present to your immediate *what is*.

To repeat: those three breaths can make a big difference in your life because they can move you from feeling as though

you have no choice but to react, to knowing that you can create enough inner spaciousness to refocus your attention in positive ways. You can then choose your responses. You can speak kindly rather than hurtfully; take your time rather than rush unnecessarily; savor the moment rather than miss the nuances of the experiences available to you.

Breath Focusing-Tension Releasing, Even Shorter Form

Step 1: Notice Tension

- You notice you're tensing and becoming reactive to your thoughts or to some external trigger.

- Remind yourself, "I'm getting triggered."

Step 2: Anchor on Your Breath

- Anchor on your breath and then breathe in a long, slow breath through your nose.

Step 3: Release Tension

- Exhale fully through your nostrils or slightly pursed lips and soften your fingers and toes.

- As you do this, coach yourself firmly by saying, "Drop it" or "Release." Imagine you are dropping a hot potato.

Step 4: Refocus

- Refocus on the present by paying attention to physical sensations such as the quality of the air on your face, smells, the contact of your feet on the floor, the texture of fabric. Notice the details of your surroundings, such as colors and shapes, plants, or paintings. Attend to any sounds.

- Remind yourself of what really matters to you when you are feeling calm and clear-headed.

Practice the Long Form BFTR technique when you have time to relax during the day or before you go to bed so that your bodymind becomes thoroughly familiar with each of the steps and how you feel when you do them. Practice with small upsets so that the technique will be available to you when the big ones come. These techniques are called practices because, to be useful to you, you'll need to practice them regularly.

AN EXERCISE

- Jot down where and when in your day you find yourself getting tense.

- Now imagine yourself using a BFTR technique to relax your bodymind in those situations. Can you feel the difference using this skill will make in your life?

Here's an example of how practicing the Breath Focusing-Tension Releasing technique helped a worried man make a difference in his life and the life of his family:

John's Story

John looked uncomfortable and a bit sheepish. He had just told me that he had come to counselling because his partner, Pete, said he had to "do something, and fast." Pete wanted John to tell me that he was "grouchy and unreasonable in his expectations of cleanliness around the house and with the kids." I asked John what he thought of that and what he wanted. He said, "Well, actually, I agree with Pete. I am grouchy and unreasonable at home. I've tried to back off, but I get really pissed off by the mess and the noise. Pete's had to put up with a lot lately. I used to be more patient. Yeah, and I'm okay with a counselling session or two—if you think it'll help make a difference." I asked John what else was going on in his life. It turned out that for months he'd had an ongoing conflict with a co-worker he believed was undermining him professionally. In addition, his elderly parents were struggling to maintain their independence following his father's stroke and it had become clear to John and his siblings that the time had come to look for an alternative living arrangement for them. John had a lot on his plate! He described Pete as being "a really incredible partner" and said he wanted to do what he could to "clean up his act" at home.

From John's comment about coming for "one or two" counselling sessions, I didn't know if I'd be seeing him again. I wanted to offer him something he could start to use right away to help him calm himself and reconnect to his more patient self. That something was the Breath Focusing-Tension Releasing technique.

Once he'd learned the mechanics of the technique and had noticed himself feeling calmer after doing it, I asked John to remember and visualize three different troubling scenarios, one at a time: one from home, one from work, and one from the situation with his parents. In each, I asked him to notice when he started to tense up and encouraged him to intervene with the Long Form BFTR technique. I encouraged him to take his time and to stay with it until he could feel calmer and more relaxed. Because of his experiences with playing team sports and coaching his son's team, John was very open to the suggestion that he combine self-coaching with his new relaxation skill.

With his home visualization, John described imagining opening the front door, seeing a pile of unfolded laundry on the sofa, and said, "Right then, it's over." I reminded him that it used to be "Right then, it's over." and now it's "Notice the tension, drop the laundry trigger and Breath Focus-Tension Release!" John decided that the most attention-getting thing for him to say to himself after that was, "God, I truly do love my family!" This made him laugh and lightened his mood. He really meant it!

During his second visualization, John felt his tension rise when he imagined hearing his supervisor praise his co-worker for work that was originally his. This situation infuriated John even as he imagined it. He could feel his outrage. I coached him to remind himself that "No matter how unjust and unfair this situation is, this stress simply isn't helping or changing the situation. And it's really tough on my body." John took the major step of dropping the trigger of "unjust, unfair" and turned to Breath Focusing-Tension Releasing. He learned to coach himself effectively by saying, "I will find ways to address this issue. I won't work myself up. I'll take strategic, meaningful action. I commit to myself to do that." We ran out of time in that first session to review the situation with his parents, but by the end of our hour John had brightened and said he felt "hopeful."

John did come back for several more sessions. At his second session, he reported that he had used the BFTR technique "a lot" and said, "I'm not sure if that had anything to do with it, but it was a lot smoother week." Pete called and left a message on my answering machine saying, "I don't know what you're doing in those counselling sessions, but whatever it is, it's working! Thank you." What was happening was that I offered something useful, and John took it and made it his own. He was willing and committed to change. He learned skills that worked for him, and he practiced them over and over.

Sometimes we don't try a new activity because it feels overwhelming to incorporate one more thing into our busy day. The BFTR techniques are custom-made for busy people.

It's important that you find and use a relaxation method that works for you.

Here is a breath-focusing technique used by Navy SEALs before they go into tough assignments (www.sealfit.com).

EXERCISE 2.2 Box Breathing

To learn this technique, make sure you are in a private, quiet spot.

Sit in your chair with a straight spine. Have both feet on the floor. Before practicing Box Breathing, read or listen to the exercise completely, and as you do, visualize yourself creating a box with your breath.

Step 1: Settling In

- Close your eyes or, if you aren't comfortable doing that, soften and lower your gaze.

- Place your hands, one on top of the other, just below your belly button. When you breathe in, imagine that you are sending your breath under and behind your hands.

Step 2: Counting

- Imagine that you are creating a box with your breath, as on an inhalation you breathe in through your nose and say silently to yourself, "In—2, 3, 4" (there's one side of the box). Hold your breath and say silently, "Hold—2, 3, 4" (that's the top of the box). Exhale (through your mouth, slightly pursed lips) and say silently to yourself, "Out—2, 3, 4" (there's the third side of the box). Then hold your breath and say silently to yourself, "Hold—2, 3, 4" (and there's the bottom of the box). Repeat the Box Breath three times.

If breathing, holding, exhaling, and holding to the count of four is too strenuous for you, start with a count of two and increase the counting sequence with practice.

Once learned, you can use this breath technique, with eyes open, to calm yourself if you start to get tense when you are out and about.

BREATH TIP

Breath expert Dr. Stig Severinsen (www.breathology.com) teaches that a 1:2 ratio (inhalation to exhalation) is most effective for relaxation. He says to inhale through your nose and exhale through either your nose or mouth. So, for a relaxing breath, if you chose to inhale to a count of four, he suggests you would exhale to a count of eight. Experiment and experience what works best for you.

EXERCISE 2.3 Mini-Breaks

Some suggestions for tension-managing, relaxation-promoting mini-breaks:

- Practice checking your hands, fingers, feet, and toes for "hanging on" or "putting on the brakes" and soften and relax them if they are clenched or tight.

- Throughout the day, tune into your breath and on your exhalation soften and say to yourself, "Releasing, letting go of tension, coming into the present" in a soft internal whisper. Do this three times in a row.

- Shift your perspective. Imagine yourself having a bird's-eye view. See yourself as one of many people, all with desires and fears, living their lives as best they can. Think of what will and will not matter to you in a year, ten years, twenty years.

- Create a list for yourself of activities you find relaxing, enjoyable, energizing, or inspiring. Incorporate at least one of these activities into your daily schedule. Consider this as important as brushing your teeth.

- Allow yourself to become completely absorbed in an enjoyable activity, like listening to music, cutting up a piece of fruit, or petting your dog, even if just for a moment or two. Then expand the time you spend absorbed in activities you enjoy.

- When you sit in a chair, take a moment to focus on allowing yourself to be fully present and to feel completely supported. Focus on the sensation of your weight on the chair and your feet on the floor.

- If you find you're walking along worrying—thinking unhelpful, anxiety-provoking thoughts—switch your focus to *camera viewing*. Describe the colors, shapes, lines, and patterns you see around you, silently to yourself, in detail, as though your eyes are the lens of a camera.

- Stretch. Move your body. Make this a go-to.

By teaching your bodymind to 're-laaax' using one of the BFTR techniques or Box Breathing, you can support yourself in stressful situations. You can shift your state—how you're feeling, what you're thinking, and your mood—by choosing thoughts, attitudes, or activities that are self-supporting (like Mini-Breaks). You can enjoy new default inner experiences of calm vitality, pleasant anticipation, interest, and curiosity.

Benefits that are worth the repetitions and slight changes in your routine!

CHAPTER 3: YOUR LIVING GOALS

"Would you tell me, please, which way I ought to go from here?" "That depends a good deal on where you want to get to." *~Lewis Carroll*

Many people go through life like Alice in Wonderland, not much caring where they go, hoping to get somewhere. To make the changes you want, to move from your *here* to your *there*, it'll be helpful for you to answer variations on the questions you ask at the beginning of any journey: Where am I starting from and where do I want to go? What is my best-case outcome? What habits will I be leaving behind for me to fully support my peace of mind and well-being? What resources do I have that I can take with me? What steps will I take to get from here to there and how will I know when I've arrived?

First, let's look at what concerns may have brought you to read this book or listen to the audio. You may be fed up with a self-defeating habit of yours or bored to death by a tired old drama you keep replaying. You may long for more clarity and vitality. You may notice that you have anxiety about the state of the world. You may be upset with a change at work and want a different job. You may be ready to leave a miserable relationship or want to revitalize a valued marriage. You may be living through an unwanted change and feel resentful, lost, or confused. You may be feeling inspired by the example of a friend who is living her personal dream. Whatever your motivation, you want a different experience in your life. You may want to focus on inner shifts. You may want to create external changes. Whichever your focus is, you want to let go of internal agitation and develop peace of mind.

Change of any kind will involve a period of inner transition. That's the getting from *here* to *there* part and will require your willingness to live with uncertainty, and your patience, determination, and trust in the process.

For example, say you have been feeling anxious, and one of your goals is to feel peaceful. You practice the exercises described in this book wholeheartedly and notice, after a week or two, to your surprise, that one morning you feel peaceful for ten minutes. Bingo. Right there for those ten minutes, your life was transformed. For that time, you achieved your goal of inner peace. You now have a strong clue that you're on track and heading in the right direction. Remind yourself of what inner peace felt like and keep practicing for more of those moments.

Often people know what they want in their lives. Most people want peace of mind, more energy, and better relationships. They want to feel that they're living purposeful, meaningful lives. They want to have a sense of connection and belonging. They want a sense of security and well-being.

Most external goals—a new house, a new relationship, travel, more money—are made with the aim of creating such inner results.

In this chapter, you'll be invited to describe the inner experience you expect your external goals to bring. You'll learn how to move in the direction of having more of your desired inner experiences regardless of your current external circumstances.

In this chapter, you'll also discover how you can use your feelings and goals as moment-to-moment guides to tell yourself when your choices are taking you in the direction of personal well-being as you are defining it or to alert you to when you are straying off your course. You'll learn about some of the inner blocks that have kept you from achieving what you say you want in your life.

Here is an example of a man clarifying his goals and learning how to use them to guide his choices:

Franks's Story

Frank came into my office clearly upset. His whole world had just been turned upside down. During a bitter argument two weeks before, his live-in girlfriend of four years had told him that she had stayed with him over the past three years only because he had provided her with financial stability while she went to university. Now that she had her degree, she was moving on.

Frank was devastated. He set his first goal as "Trudy wants to be with me." I told him that while that might be what he wanted, it's not something he had control over. Frank didn't like that he couldn't insist, convince or coerce Trudy to want to stay with him, but he understood the self-responsibility principle and agreed to shift his goal. He chose the goal of being "honorable" in his interactions with Trudy. His longer-term goal was "to be in a mutually loving, committed relationship." When Frank found himself wanting to punish Trudy, he would remind himself of his commitment to himself to be honorable in his dealings with her. And while he did slip up and have a yelling match with her shortly after setting his goals, he was able to pull himself back from totally giving in to his impulse to scream insults at her. He was able to get himself back on track. When he questioned if he could ever trust another woman, he'd remind himself of his goal to eventually be in a mutually loving relationship with a woman. He'd then remind himself not to generalize Trudy's behavior to all women.

As we worked together, Frank began to let go and grieve the loss of what he had thought he had with Trudy. His self-respect grew with his ability to monitor and manage his reactions.

Frank was surprised to notice that as he took responsibility for his own thoughts and behaviors in the relationship, he began to feel some compassion for Trudy. He stayed in alignment with what he wanted for himself and thus made it more likely that eventually, he would be available for the kind of relationship he yearned for. With patience, perseverance, and self-compassion, he gradually shifted from living with emotional turmoil to developing acceptance and even enjoyment in his current circumstance. He started to anticipate having a positive future.

Here's an example of a young woman taking responsibility in setting and using her goals to keep herself on track:

Miriam's Story

Miriam, an IT professional in her late twenties, lived with her parents, whom she described as "really great, but too interested in my life and too bossy." Miriam firmly believed that she had absolutely no other choice than to live with her parents because she was working her way out of major credit card debt, and they had said she could live with them rent-free for a year. She felt grateful for her parents' generosity, resentful of what felt to her like their smothering attention, and guilty about her resentment.

Initially, Miriam wanted her counselling goal to be that her parents would understand her desire to be "treated with respect as an independent adult." Because Miriam was clear that she was not going to move out of her parent's home, I suggested that a more self-responsible goal could be to develop her own inner experience of peace, purpose, and independence while living in harmony with her parents. Miriam thought that sounded unlikely, but that it was a good place to start.

Miriam learned that she could keep herself on track toward her goal of feeling independent and purposeful while living at home by frequently reminding herself (not her parents) that she was an adult with a wide circle of friends, many skills, work she liked, and a rapidly disappearing debt load. She firmly and kindly coached herself when she felt resentful of her parents' behavior, saying to herself that it was her choice to stay in their home to pay off her debt. She reminded herself frequently how wonderful and free she'd feel to be rid of her debt. She visualized moving into her own apartment and starting to save. She learned to recognize when she reverted to adolescent behavior and during our sessions rehearsed ways she could remain adult in her relationship with her parents. She used a Breath Focusing-Tension Releasing technique when she noticed herself tensing and feeling reactive. She used her goals as her compass and enjoyed her developing sense of autonomy.

EXERCISE 3.1 Clarifying and Aligning Your Goals and Values

Choose a place where you are comfortable and won't be interrupted for forty-five minutes to an hour. The exercise that follows involves a six-step process.

Have your favorite writing materials with you. If you usually use a computer, you might experiment with switching to using pen or colored pencils and paper to see if you notice any difference in your process or creativity.

Settle in and take three relaxed breaths, imagining that as you inhale through your nose that your breath pours into your pelvic bowl. Feel your weight being held by the chair and how the soles of your feet connect with the ground. As you exhale gently through your nose or your slightly pursed mouth, imagine tension flowing out on your breath.

Read through or listen to the entire assignment right to Old Guard Objections before writing so that you have a sense of the flow of the work.

Read and write—perhaps a bulleted list, a poem, a prose piece, or a series of descriptions. Take your time. Go into detail. This is you mapping out the shape, texture, and flavor of your life.

If you find yourself writing a negatively stated goal such as, "My goal is not to feel so boxed in." use that negative "not to feel" as an invitation to write what you do want, as in, "I do want to feel like I have choices, like I am freer inside." If your goal is to stop hating your body, use "stop hating" as a springboard to what you do want. Shift your goal to "My goal is to accept and appreciate my body." If that seems too much, try "My goal is to tolerate and be kind to my body." Turn what you don't want inside out, to tell yourself what you do want.

Your energy flows in the direction of your focus.

When you focus your attention and energy on what you do want, and away from what you don't want, you create a powerful internal shift. So powerful that you may notice your mind coming up with many reasons why your newly stated goal is impossible. For now, just notice this mind chatter, refocus on your breath, and go back to this goal setting exercise. Do this noticing and refocusing as many times as necessary.

Step 1: What Do I Want?

Are you like Frank used to be, believing that your life will change for the better only if someone else changes? Now is the time to shift your focus away from that other person and onto yourself.

You may say to yourself, "But I don't know what I want. I don't know what to do to feel better" If that's the case, think about what you do know you want and like. Most of us want good health and peace of mind. Feel that knowing in your body. How do you decide what to have for breakfast? Which clothes to wear? What book to read or movie to see? Whether or not to watch the news? Who to share your time with? Paying attention to your subtle *movements toward* and *movements away from* will give you clues about how to tune in to your preferences and desires. Becoming more consciously aware of them can help you decide what you want for yourself.

The idea is to begin to move in the direction of thoughts, feelings, ways of being, and activities that are congruent with what you want your future self to experience. Clues that you're on track are that you're feeling engaged and energized and probably challenged.

- Start by asking yourself: What do I really want for myself? If I was thriving in my life what would be changed? If so, how? How would I be feeling? What would I be doing differently? Would my life be transformed? If so, how?

- Breathe, release tension on your exhalation, and write freely, without censoring yourself.

Now shift your body—even just a slight movement, perhaps a small twist of your spine—and breathe deeply.

Release your breath with a sigh and start fresh.

Explore these questions:

- If I could transform my life, what would I want to change? How do I want to feel? How do I want to live? What would the quality of my relationships be? Do I want to contribute to the world in some bigger way? What would that look like? What do I want to bring to the world? Is there a project or poem, adventure, aspiration or exploration that I have tucked away or denied? Who other than me might notice changes in my life? Who will celebrate with me? This might be someone you have yet to meet, or it may be a good friend who wants the best for you.

When you feel complete with what you've written so far, stretch and shift. Breathe into your pelvis and release your breath consciously. Gaze around the room.

- Now ask yourself: Is there something I long for? Something I deeply desire? Is there some whisper in me that I have chosen to ignore that I might want to acknowledge now and include in my writings? When I am very old and look back on my life, what am I going to be grateful to myself for having felt, seen, said, done, been, contributed?

- Breathe in, breathe out, and write. These questions are designed to help you move from your familiar responses into less-explored territory.

Finish up this section with a round of the short form of the Breath Focusing-Tension Releasing technique.

Congratulations. You now have an expanded vision of the direction you want to take your life. You can return to this exercise to update your vision at any time. Now it's time to ask yourself what your answers to these questions tell you about your underlying motivation and what you value.

You might be asking yourself "What does all this have to do with me supporting my peace of mind and personal well-being? Using a researcher's attitude of interest and curiosity notice the contrast between how you feel when you make your choices based on what you truly value and how you feel when you know you've made a choice that is incongruent with what matters to you. It's the difference between feeling calm, confident, and clear and feeling out-of-alignment, "off," and uneasy.

Step 2: Your Values

After the example of Kendra's Story that follows this description, you'll be asked to unearth what deeply motivates you by completing each of the two following sentences three times:

- **First:** "This goal is important to me because__________"

- **Second:** "When I achieve this goal, I'll feel__________"

- **Third**: Once you're aware of *why* you're motivated to achieve your goal and how you'll *feel* when your goal is achieved, you'll ask yourself the following questions: What *choices* will I make when I've met my goal? What *actions* will I take when I've met my goal? What more does this tell me about what I value?

Journal your thoughts throughout this exercise.

Here is an example of a woman living her values:

Kendra's Story

Doing this exercise Kendra decided her goal was to buy a house. She decided it was important to her because she didn't want to have to worry about her landlord selling her home, she wanted freedom to make structural changes if she wanted to, and she wanted to have pets without asking a landlord for permission.

Kendra valued her security, independence, and freedom to choose. She believed that when she achieved her goal of home ownership, she'd feel secure, relieved, and responsible.

When she thought about feeling that way, she realized that, as a homeowner, she would have the opportunity to contribute to her community in a way that felt meaningful to her—by sharing her home with a refugee family—something that had been a dream of hers since high school. So, in meeting her goal of owning her own home, Kendra will fulfill a long-standing dream of supporting a refugee family; she'll be contributing meaningfully to her community, and she'll be an inspiration to the young women she plans to mentor.

Kendra values community, contribution, and keeping her commitments to herself.

By attending deeply to your *why* you'll be able to hone in on what underlies your motivation—your values. Knowing what you value, what matters most to you, will impact how you choose to use your precious time.

Feel your weight on the chair, your feet on the floor. Take a relaxing breath and let yourself delve into this next series of questions.

- For each one of your goals, complete the following sentences three times, like this: "This goal is important to me because_______and it's important because_______and it's important to me because_______."

- Take your time and feel that knowing in your body.

- Then complete the following sentence for each goal: "When I achieve this goal, I'll feel__________and I'll feel__________and I will also feel__________."

- Pause to breathe in each of these feelings. For example, if one of your words is "free" think of a time you felt free, even for a moment, and breathe in that expansive feeling.

- Now ask yourself for each goal, "When I've *met* this goal, what *choices* will I make and what *actions* will I take? What more does this tell me about what I value?

- Acknowledge the empowerment available to you.

Pause to imagine your breath entering and leaving your body like a cleansing wave, starting through the soles of your feet and rising to the top of your head. Hold it there briefly. Exhale down from the top of your head, imagining your breath gently sweeping through your body and leaving through the soles of your feet. Feel your weight on the chair, your feet on the floor.

You may discover as you do this part of the exercise that a goal you thought was important isn't congruent with your consciously held values. This may feel like a dilemma, but it can also be an opportunity to develop more clarity about what matters most to you now. You may find something that was important to you years ago has faded away, replaced by a more current goal and up-to-date value.

Knowing why your goals are important to you and acting on that awareness will motivate you to stay on track with yourself.

Don't worry if you get stuck. Just write what comes to you and then move on. You can return to this exercise many times.

Step 3: Focusing In

Now's the time to ask yourself, "To get the results that I want from reading this book and doing all the exercises, which one or two of my goals do I want to focus on over the next six weeks?"

- Choose a goal or goals that you can reach by committing to taking small, consistent daily steps and following through with them.

- Write your goal or goals for the next six weeks. Write in the present tense as though you have already accomplished your goals and add a positive emotion. Switch "In six weeks I don't want to feel so anxious" to "I enjoy feeling calm and peaceful" or "I'm delighted to have inner peace." If your goal is longer term, such as to get out of debt, choose a six-week goal that will start you moving in that direction. "In six weeks I'll have a plan in place to eliminate my debt and will have embarked on that plan." Use your creative imagination to evoke the feelings you want when you achieve your goal.

- Notice with interest and curiosity your thoughts and feelings as you do this.

- Once you have written your goals in the present tense, get up and take a short break. Have a glass of water. Stretch and feel your breath deepen.

After your break, once again make sure that you're comfortable and have privacy before you move on.

Step 4: Experience What You Want Right Now

"But," you may say, "How can I experience what I want right now? I'm not there yet. I don't have a clue what that would be like!"

Let's take a look at the goal of feeling calm. Has there ever been a time when you felt even a glimmer of what it might be like to feel calm and peaceful? A hint? A moment? That's it! Right there, in that remembering, you have a felt experience of inner calm, however fleeting and faint. That's what you want to imagine and expand. That faintly familiar feeling of how you feel when you are calm.

Your next question might be, "Why should I bother to do this?"

The answer is that what you believe is real and possible for yourself dramatically impacts your results in the world, especially when you vividly imagine and feel your goals as already accomplished.

- For each of your goals, immerse yourself as much as you can, head to toe, in how you will feel when you have reached it. If you find yourself saying, "Yeah, but my life is such a contrast to that, it only makes me feel bad." smile at yourself and say kindly, gently and firmly, "I'm willing to learn a new way, starting now" and refocus on this exercise.

- Vividly imagine how you'll feel, the sounds you'll hear, your sensations, what you'll see and what you'll be doing when you achieve each goal.

- Saturate yourself in the experience of having what you want in your life. Hear it; feel it; see it; taste it; smell it; feel your emotions—now. You're letting your bodymind become familiar, in the here and now, with the experience of what you want in your life as though it has already happened.

- If you just can't feel what you want to bring into your life right now, take the time to imagine as vividly as possible what a difference living your goals will make in your life.

- You could make a dream board to visually represent your goals; or a mind-movie (www.mindmovie.com) as a vivid reminder of what you want in your life.

After imagining living your goals in the present, ask yourself, with curiosity and interest, "What qualities do

I need to develop and embody to bring what I want into my life? Courage? Kindness? Determination? Patience? Steadfastness? Trust?" As you develop these qualities, you support yourself to be the person you need to become to create the life you want for yourself.

Finish the following sentence: "The qualities I am choosing to develop and embody are: _______________________________."

Step 5: Commit to Your Goals

A more accurate way of saying this is: commit to yourself.

- Let's say your goal is "to have inner peace." Say to yourself, "I commit to myself that I will create inner peace" or "I commit to myself to learn to do what it takes to create inner peace." If your inner doubter challenges these statements, simply notice any tension in your body and do a short form of the BFTR technique. Return to this exercise.

- Take time now to write out your commitments to yourself for each of your goals.

Intend these results for yourself. Think of having an intention as casting a strong guideline to follow to your desired future.

Step 6: Your Living Goals

Use your goals as your inner compass to keep yourself on track choice by choice as you move toward creating a fulfilling life of inner peace, well-being, and thriving for yourself.

Without taking this step, goal setting is just an interesting exercise.

Here's how to do that: Ask yourself these important questions when you are in an uncomfortable moment or are noticing the temptation of an old habit:

- Is what I am doing, feeling, or thinking right now, in this moment, taking me toward or away from what I know will support my total well-being?

- Is the way I am reacting right now taking me toward or away from my best-case outcome or what I want to bring to the world? What do I want to embody? Is there something I can do, say or think differently to stay on track with what I know really matters to me?

- Is there a way I can stay in integrity with myself and choose a different attitude or approach here?

It is in these moment-to-moment decisions that you create your life.

Remind yourself that you chose your goals. Nobody external to you is forcing you to achieve them.

- Read your goals, write them out, feel them as real, and refresh your commitment to yourself in the morning, regularly during the day, and before you go to bed at night to get maximum benefit from these exercises.

Take time to acknowledge yourself for having gained clarity on what you want for yourself in your life, for understanding why this is important to you, and for having made the commitment to yourself to develop the inner qualities you will need to achieve your goals.

This is the end of Part 1 and it's a good time to pause. Take a break. Go for a walk. Bounce on your trampoline if you have one. Stretch. Drink water. Refresh yourself.

You may decide that this is enough writing for today, or you may want to carry on.

When you're ready to re-engage with this material, make sure that you have half an hour of uninterrupted time and privacy before you continue. Give yourself the gift of your focused attention.

Make sure you're comfortable and have water or another favorite non-alcoholic drink close by.

Have your writing materials and your written goals with you.

Take three relaxed breaths, and, as you gently exhale, imagine that tension flows out on your breath. Relax your fingers and toes. Come present as you feel the weight of your body on your chair and where the soles of your feet connect with the ground.

Read or listen to the Old Guard Objections preamble and the Outdated Belief exercises before writing.

EXERCISE 3.2 Old Guard Objections

The internal grumbling, muttering, and objections you may have noticed as you stated your goals provide a glimpse into what has kept you from already having the life you want. (For example: "This will never work." "This is ridiculous." "It'll work for everyone else, not me." "It's too hard.")

Taken together, they reveal the blocks you've created that have held you back from feeling deeply satisfied and nourished by your choices. They give clues to the limiting beliefs (not truths) that you have developed throughout your life about yourself, others, and the world around you, and through which you filter your experiences. You learned these limiting beliefs from your caregivers, siblings, teachers, and classmates, from the media, from a myriad of influences. A way of thinking about these objections is to think of them as the voice of your Inner Old Guard trying to keep you safe. Ironically, this apparent safety is often simply familiar, and can be uncomfortable, restricting, and limiting.

As you do the exercises in this book, you will be asking yourself to evolve new ways of thinking, feeling, behaving, and being.

Because we are biological beings with alarm responses designed for the survival of our long-ago ancestors, setting new goals for yourself may feel as though you're stepping outside the safety of companionship and campfire into unknown territory. A primitive part of your brain may trigger a red alert leading you to feel anxious, overwhelmed, or like quitting the exercises. Use one of the Breath Focusing-Tension Releasing techniques or Box Breathing to support yourself when you feel stressed about trying new ways. Coach yourself with compassion. You can do this.

Step 1: Acknowledge Outdated Beliefs

- Read your six-week goal or goals from the previous exercise.

- Notice in a matter-of-fact way the internal objections that come up as you read each one.

Important: If it is difficult for you to do this exercise. and you feel at risk or deeply unsettled, consider that you may be reacting to past trauma. If you have unprocessed trauma in your system, and your bodymind goes into high red alert—and/or—if you feel unsafe doing this or any exercise, please do not continue. Practice self-compassion and patience and find professional support.

- If you are ready to continue, write out any objections. For example, if a goal of yours is to start dating, notice how you might say to yourself, "Oh, it'll never work for me, I'm too short/fat/old/incompetent/shy/lazy."

- For each goal ask yourself at least three times "What else have I believed that has slowed me down or kept me from reaching this goal?"

- Take your time with these questions. Breathe.

Don't believe your objections. Often, they are so familiar they feel like just the way it is. By recognizing them and writing them out in this exercise, you have the opportunity to be clear about their false messages, challenge them, shift how you feel, and move on. Your job is to name the Inner Old Guard objectively.

Remember, you're witnessing an ancient part of your brain that is alert for danger, that doesn't like the unknown, that is trying to keep you from being hurt, or from being in danger of annihilation. You are accessing the internal programming (beliefs, not truths) that has held you back from achieving your goals.

Step 2: Counter and Release Outdated Beliefs

- Once you have written down all the objections you have to a particular goal, pick an objection ("I'm too tall/skinny/young/awkward." or "It's too hard.") and say it out loud.

- Notice how you feel in your body. Do you feel an increase in tension in any area, a constriction, a subtle shift in your posture, a numbing, an increase in heart rate? You may notice a familiar emotional state, such as feeling defeated or discouraged, when you state your old belief to yourself. Just notice this with interest and curiosity. You're creating the opportunity for yourself to acknowledge default emotional states and the impact of your old beliefs on your body tension.

- Notice in a matter-of-fact way if you are tempted to build a case for the old belief as in, "Yeah, I really am too dumb/tired/scared." Shift your focus to anchor on your breath. Continue the exercise.

- Say kindly, out loud if you have privacy, to the Old Guard belief, "Thank you for trying to keep me safe in the past. I'm in charge and I'm learning powerful new ways now. I'm capable, able, and resilient."

- On your inhalation, imagine you are breathing soothing balm gently into any tightness or holding you may notice. On your exhalation imagine tension releasing through your relaxed fingers and toes, on your breath, and through your pores. Say softly to yourself. "I release the tension you bring. I'm done with it! Releasing this tension, letting it go. I'm coming fully, vitally present in my bodymind."

You are using your powerful imagination for your well-being.

- Do this for several breaths without any expectation of a particular result. A helpful attitude will be simply to notice with kindness and compassion.

- Go through your objections for each of your goals, reading them aloud and attending to whatever tension and emotional habits you notice. Use the thank-you statement, your tension-releasing breath, your countering statement and coming fully into the present for each.

You'll have the opportunity many times to observe, counter and release tension as these old habitual beliefs resurface, trying to get your attention as you experiment with new ways of being.

Important: If you start to notice yourself believing the old limiting beliefs, just move along to the next goal, or stop doing this exercise for now and return to it after you have done the exercises in Chapters 4, 5, and 6.

It may be that as you read one of your goals, you feel expansive, enthusiastic, and excited. Just notice this with interest. Stay with these vital, potent feelings for as long as they last. Saturate yourself and enjoy, but don't hang on. When they shift, go on to your next goal. You can revisit these feelings when you re-read your goals to inspire and motivate yourself to stay with the plan you have set for yourself.

You are now more aware of the limiting beliefs that come up as you move out of your familiar comfort zone.

When an outdated belief rears its constricting head, such as "Danger is everywhere. I must be hyper-alert;" you can say, "Oh, I recognize you. You're a limiting belief and you are no longer relevant in my life. I am resourceful and resilient. I can realistically assess for danger and look after myself now. I know I am safe enough. I choose to release you."

Then check your body to see if you are holding familiar tension and, if so, observe it with kindness, and breathe into that area. Imagine surrounding the tension with soothing warmth on your inhalation, and the tightness softening and releasing as you exhale. After you have done that, refocus on your surroundings and carry on. Do this as often as the old, tired, out-of-date stories come up.

Old Guard Objections, Short Form

Step 1: Recognize and acknowledge the out-of-date, limiting belief.

Step 2: On your inhalation say: "Oh, it's you."

Step 3: On your exhalation say: "Goodbye."

Step 4: Refocus on your immediate surroundings, or on what matters most to you in the present.

If you're consistent and wholehearted with this practice, you'll notice that there will be longer and longer periods between visitations!

In Chapter 8, Time Traveling, you'll learn an additional effective method for releasing painful, limiting beliefs.

Reward yourself for having more clarity on the values that underlie the goals you've chosen. You've come to a compassionate understanding of why and how you've limited yourself in the past. You've learned effective ways to counter and release outdated beliefs and have been introduced to practices that can transform your self-limiting fears. You can use the BFTR techniques that you learned in Chapter 2 to create inner spaciousness so that rather than reacting in old familiar ways, you can pause, then consciously make life-affirming choices that are in alignment with your current values and goals. Treat yourself to your favorite cup of tea. Light a candle and have a bath. Go for a run. Talk with a friend. Cuddle with your sweetie. Celebrate!

CHAPTER 4: LIGHTENING UP

"Gratitude is heaven itself." *~William Blake*

I have a friend who travels lightly. I'm in awe of her ability to dress elegantly for a variety of occasions, seemingly out of thin air. I used to stagger under the weight of my two overstuffed just-in-case bags, feeling harried and as though I had forgotten to bring something. From my friend's example, I discovered the ease that comes with packing systematically and lightly.

The next step of your journey toward consistently supporting your peace of mind, well-being—and thriving—is to acknowledge the gifts, strengths, blessings, and resources that are already yours. What's in your bags that can enrich and lighten your journey? What can you leave behind?

You may automatically see the best in others but discount your own talents. You may be someone who, when you are complimented, feels uncomfortable and quickly deflects the attention. Now is the time to acknowledge your gifts even if you don't feel resourceful. Now is the time to remember that you do have skills, talents, and abilities, inner and outer. It's time for you to name and own them.

Find an hour of private time and settle in with your favorite pen and paper, or computer.

As you do the following exercises, you might want to create a very personal journal to return to again and again. Enjoy adding drawings, pictures or poems to your Resource Reminder.

Breathe three soft, easy, relaxing breaths; as you exhale, allow your body to soften.

Do you feel the weight of your body on the chair? Can you let the chair support you?

What thoughts and feelings do you notice coming up when you think of doing this exercise? Just notice with interest.

EXERCISE 4.1 Your Resource Inventory

Start by reading or listening through to Exercise 4.2, then begin to develop your Resource Inventory.

Step 1: Questions

Write down those aspects of your life, inner and outer, that help nourish, sustain, and support you. I'm going to offer questions as jumping-off points for your exploration. You may have other questions.

Write without censoring. Please don't judge what you write. No buts allowed!

Don't feel you have to answer all the questions.

- What internal qualities do you have that you like? For example, are you curious, grateful, kind? Are you compassionate, thoughtful, and willing? Are you persistent? Fun-loving? Loyal? Quirky? Empathetic? Reserved? Name them all.

- Think of someone you know who likes, respects, or loves you. What would they say about your excellent qualities? Add those qualities to your list.

You may find this exercise challenging. You may not have had a supportive person in your life. This may feel like blowing your own horn. It may feel indulgent or selfish to focus on yourself in this way. What is actually happening is that you're learning to acknowledge yourself, much as you would acknowledge a friend.

You may be someone who just doesn't like yourself very much. See if you can find at least three words to describe yourself at your best. Perhaps a time when you were generous, thoughtful, and kind?

- Deep breath and jot them down.

If you get stuck, you might think of a friend or acquaintance of yours and the qualities they have that you like, respect, or admire. Do you have similar qualities? Usually, we admire and recognize in others qualities that we already have or have the capacity for, or would like to develop, in ourselves.

More questions:

- Do you have a safe place? Is there a place in nature where you like to walk? Is there a lake, a hill, a rock where you feel connected to yourself, the land, the larger world? These are all resources for you.

- Do you have childhood memories that support and nourish you?

Here's an example of a childhood experience that's a resource for me now:

Susan's Story

As a child I had the freedom to explore, with my dog, the woods and lakeshore around the little cabin my father built. I swam and wandered unsupervised for hours.

I like to think of myself as having been an adventurous child enjoying nature. This has

***carried forward in my life as an appreciation
and love for the natural world, and for dogs.
I'm resourced by these memories.***

More questions:

- Do you have children? If so, how has being a parent stretched your awareness of your abilities and resourcefulness? If not, what do you most like about how you've been with the children or animals in your life? What have you created and nurtured?

Notice if you are drawn to slip into parental guilt—"I could have done better;" or to guilt or regret about not having had a child. Kindly bring yourself back to this exercise.

- What are your skills—at home, at work, in relationships? What do you do just because you love doing it? What do your friends say you do well? Are you a good listener? Where are you a leader? Where are you a supportive follower? What do you appreciate about how you care for others? How do you contribute—to your family? friends? community?

- Do you engage in activities that bring you joy? If so, what are they? Are you creative? Describe your creativity. If you don't think of yourself as being creative, what are some of the ways you express yourself in the world? What would you like to know more about? What piques your interest?

If these questions resonate with you, your answers are your resources.

- Do you feel passionate about an activity? For example: Do you love gardening and having your hands in the earth? What enlivens you? Do you like to cook? Read? Build or paint things?

- How about your physical being? Do you enjoy movement? If so, in what ways? Biking? Dance? Yoga? Making love? Walking in nature? Is there a part of your body that pleases you? Do you have the great good fortune of sight, of legs that walk, of arms that reach, of hands that grasp, of a tongue that tastes?

Your body may feel like a painful burden to you. It may be difficult to find gratitude for or pleasure in your physical self. A wheelchair-bound friend gets pleasure from the feel of water on his skin when he showers. That is a resource for him.

- Can you acknowledge as a resource that your body is doing the best it can for you? Write about the resourcefulness you have in your body.

- You may feel isolated and out of touch with people. Think back in your life—was there ever a teacher, an aunt or uncle, or a family friend who let you know that he or she recognized and appreciated your uniqueness? This memory can be a resource for you now.

- You may share a nodding acquaintance with someone that helps you feel part of the human community. That relationship is a resource of yours.

- What relationships do you have? Are there people in your life who provide you with support, backup, caring, acknowledgment, appreciation? Do you have people in your life who know and accept you, just as you are?

- Are there people in your family ancestry to whom you can relate or whom you admire? Do you have people you consider to be your tribe? Do you belong to clubs, a choir, a spiritual community? How does your membership nourish and resource you?

- Do you create rituals by yourself, with friends, family members or a larger community that nourish you? Describe them.

- Write about your connections with the people who resource you.

- Do you have a pet or pets? If so, what does your relationship with animals offer you? Did you have a pet or pets at an earlier time in your life? How do you feel when you think of them?

For many people, a beloved pet provides welcomed acceptance and a sense of deep connection.

- What are your material resources? Do you have a home, a room? If you do, is that place a resource for you? If so, what about it do you most enjoy? What can you see from your window? Is this a resource for you? Do you bring flowers into your room and look at them with pleasure? Do you use your clothes, your jewelry, to express yourself? If so, these are resources for you. Do you have a painting, sculpture, or photograph that you look at to feel inspired or expanded? What books or movies inform you in meaningful ways? All resources.

- Write your thoughts about your material resources.

Step 2: Reviewing

Review what you've written. Whether it's a poem or document, however short or long, it can now be a resource for you. Enjoy adding to it. Read it to celebrate your riches or to remind yourself of your resourcefulness if you feel shaky, empty, or lost.

It may be that this exercise has stirred painful feelings of loss—of physical abilities, people, pets, or things you once enjoyed, and thought would be with you forever. Be kind to yourself.

Experiment with allowing those feelings, even if only for a few breaths. Then return to the present using a BFTR technique.

You can gradually build up your tolerance for staying present through uncomfortable feelings rather than getting lost in them or shutting them down. In this way, you will increase your emotional flexibility and your inner aliveness.

If this feels too challenging, shift your focus to your weight on the chair, your feet on the floor. Have a glass of water or a cup of tea.

Important: If you have suffered trauma, are experiencing PTSD, or are currently at risk, please access professional help. Go ahead to the Practicing an Attitude of Gratitude exercise further on in this chapter. Do the exercises at your own pace.

If you're tempted to tell yourself sad stories about how things used to be much better in your life, just notice this. Repetitive negative storytelling will keep you from recognizing opportunities for enjoyment, appreciation, and gratitude in your present circumstances. Your familiar sad stories, no matter how compelling, will actively erode your sense of well-being, resourcefulness, and resilience in the present. As you carry on, you will find exercises designed to help you unhook your attention from outdated storytelling.

Pause to look around. You may want to stand, stretch, and give yourself a gentle twist before you carry on to the next exercise.

Read through to, or listen to, Practicing an Attitude of Gratitude before starting Creating your Resource Reminder.

EXERCISE 4.2 Creating Your Resource Reminder

- Glance over your Resource Inventory. Notice the words or phrases you have written that resonate with you, or that appeal to you the most and write them down.

- Experiment with using those words or phrases to complete the sentence "I am______________." Say each out loud and notice how you feel.

- Now using these words or phrases, create a powerful statement about who you are as your most resourced and confident self.

Examples of resource statements are: "I am an honorable, honest, and caring man who is willing to grow. I am an excellent provider." "I am a creative, insightful, and generous woman." "I am funny, active, and intelligent and I am a valued member of my church community."

- Your powerful statement about who you are as your most resourced, confident self is: "I am a______________________."

- Say your statement out loud to yourself. Notice how you

feel when you say your statement. Have fun with it!

Keep your Resource Reminder with you to remind yourself of your strengths. Give yourself reminders, maybe post-it notes or digital memory jogs, to read your sentence during the day. Breathe in (be inspired) when you read it and give yourself time to feel the good feelings it generates.

Share your Resource Reminder only if that feels right to you. If you have someone in your life with whom you feel safe and connected, you might ask that person to read your sentence back to you if you would like to hear it from someone else. They would say, "You (your name) are (your resource reminder statement)." Breathe in to receive your statement and imagine the good feelings generated entering every cell of your body.

You can use your Resource Reminder as a guide if you are feeling shaky or off track. Read your statement and ask yourself, "How would a person with these qualities think, feel, walk, talk, breathe, behave, and be right now?" Take time to nurture and experience those qualities in yourself.

Here is an example of a woman using her Resource Reminder to support herself at work. Her Resource Reminder statement is "I am a confident, caring, generous, and worthy woman."

Sarah's Story

> *One day Sarah's supervisor, Ellen, seemed uncharacteristically distant and abrupt with her. Sarah's heart dropped at first, but she wisely decided to not take Ellen's behavior personally. She used her Resource Reminder as a mantra that day. She repeatedly asked herself "How would a confident, caring, generous, and worthy woman be thinking, feeling, behaving, right now?" whenever she slipped into self-doubt. The next day Ellen called a team meeting to talk about unexpected budget cuts, the strain she was feeling because of them, and unwanted changes that would be happening to one of their major projects.*
>
> *Sarah was grateful that she had spared herself a day and night worrying that she might have inadvertently offended her supervisor.*

Here's an example of a client setting goals and creating her Resource Inventory and Reminder.

Joan's Story

Joan is a bright, attractive lawyer. Only the dark smudge of circles under her eyes hinted at her inner distress. She was raised by two professional parents; her father was a partner in a top accounting firm and her mother was an anesthesiologist in a teaching hospital. Both parents instilled in their two daughters a strong work ethic and the belief that they could and should excel at everything they did. As children, if one of the girls brought home a grade less than perfect, they were greeted by their father's teasing, "What's this? There must be a mistake here;" and their mother's anxious, "This isn't funny; if you can't do well at school, who knows where you'll end up."

As it happened, Joan's sister, Marina, was brilliant and consistently made top marks. When Marina suffered a psychotic break in the middle of her second year of medical school, she was forced to withdraw from school permanently. The mantle of family expectations fell on Joan's shoulders. During her articling year, Joan met and married a carpenter, shocking and disappointing her parents who thought she should have married a professional man. Now a junior partner in a law firm, Joan was on track with her career goals and loved her supportive husband but was worried about her distractedness and her "dark thoughts." She had days when she just didn't want to get out of bed or bother with any of her regular activities. She was not actively suicidal, but said she found it hard to "carry on." Joan came for counselling because she and her husband were thinking of starting a family and she wanted to "straighten herself out" before she got pregnant.

Joan worked on saying what goals she did want rather than what she didn't want, even though that was foreign to her. She was convinced that if she "softened up" on herself she would lose her drive. I asked her to take a leap of faith with me and to trust the process I was suggesting. Eventually, she came up with her goals for counselling that reflected her values of physical and emotional health and strong connection with her partner: "to enjoy my life more," "to be more expressive with my husband" and "to be more physically active." She made a commitment to herself to follow through on her goals and learn the needed skills, but she was clear that she thought she should have figured this all out on her own.

When it came time to start developing her Resource Inventory, Joan grew tense. She had learned in her parents' home that while academic excellence had been expected, any acknowledgment or praise was seen as encouraging Joan to "blow her own horn" or "get puffed up," which would result in her mother "taking her down a peg." Her own excitement about her accomplishments had been met at best with reserve and at worst with sarcasm and mockery.

I encouraged Joan to take three Breath Focusing-Tension Releasing breaths, softening and relaxing on the exhalations, and asked her to remember how very different her circumstances were now that she had a home of her own. Joan did this and lost some of the tension around her eyes.

I asked her if there had been anyone in her childhood who she knew cared for her and with whom she could completely be herself. It turned out that Joan had spent many weekends with her paternal grandmother, who had adored her. In her grandmother's home, Joan had played dress-up with her cousins and had performed plays for her approving and applauding grandparents. Joan brightened remembering this early experience. It had led her to take courses in theater at university, risking her parent's disapproval.

I asked Joan to imagine how her grandmother, who had died three years previously, would have described her beloved granddaughter. Joan was off and running, developing her Resource Inventory. "Bright, imaginative, inquisitive, and, yes, silly." She added to it by imagining how her devoted husband would describe her. "Inspiring, supportive, caring, good cook, usually fun to be with." She then described the qualities she liked about herself in her marriage. "Caring and supportive but not very demonstrative." I reminded her that her Resource Inventory was not a place for "buts," so she left her list as "caring and supportive." She also said that she liked that she could be "rebellious and think outside the box."

> *Joan added that she was a "generous and supportive co-worker." She also said that she thought of herself as being "a good friend" and "quite brilliant at home decor." Joan ended up enjoying this exercise and said that she planned to add more examples to her list.*

> *Joan reviewed her Resource Inventory and came up with this Resource Reminder statement: "I am a supportive, caring, bright, risk-taking, and talented woman. I am loving and learning to express my love openly."*

Pause to take three easy, relaxing breaths.

Shift your posture.

If you feel at all thirsty, have a glass of water or a cup of herbal tea before starting the final exercise in this chapter.

EXERCISE 4.3 Practicing an Attitude of Gratitude

There's a great old blues song, written and sung by William Bell, called *You Don't Miss Your Water ('Til Your Well Runs Dry)*. A daily Gratitude Practice is a wonderful way to appreciate your water while it's there for you to drink!

Step 1: Amplifying Your Gratitude Awareness

An impactful daily gratitude practice is to start and end your day by writing down what you're grateful for in that moment, taking time to feel your gratitude in your body. Without taking time to experience, to actually feel, your gratitude, this becomes a rote exercise.

- Write three to five things you're grateful for right now.

- Take the time it takes to consciously immerse yourself in feelings of gratitude.

Your Gratitude Practice can be a nurturing, enlivening, refreshing resource for you.

- If you find yourself slow to come up with things to be grateful for, think of the natural world. Think of oxygen-giving trees. Think of how much your life has benefited by those who have gone before you. Somebody built the house that shelters you. Somebody made the clothes you wear.

- If you get stuck or are feeling in lack, ask yourself, "Are there things I could be feeling grateful for even though I don't feel it now? Can I feed my children and myself?" Gratitude. "Have I eyes to see the beauty of the sky?" Gratitude. "Friends who love me?" Gratitude. "Living, loving family members?" Gratitude.

- Still stuck? Think of all your body does for you. Think of the water that gushes out of the tap when you turn it on.

If painful thoughts come in during your Gratitude Practice, perhaps about destructive world events or perceived personal failings, simply notice your thoughts and feelings on your inhalation; on your exhalation offer whatever situation caused you pain, and yourself, a blessing for peace and healing. You could simply say, "May I be peaceful and healed. May we all be peaceful and healed. May the world be peaceful and healed" Do this for three breaths, then bring yourself back to your life-affirming Gratitude Practice.

- If you find yourself simply unable or unwilling to squeeze out gratitude today, say to yourself, "This dry spell will pass." Then say, "My intention is to be grateful."

Step 2: Gratitude Opportunities

Some additional meaningful ways you can support an attitude of gratitude are:

- As you go through your day, remind yourself that your intention is to have an ongoing attitude of gratitude. Do a regular gratitude check-in. Stay alert for thoughts of complaining or criticizing. Instead ask yourself, "Right this minute what am I grateful for? Do this when you're going about your daily life, grocery shopping, paying your rent, getting on a bus, so that it becomes a habit.

- Practice saying "I'm grateful that I have the resources to pay this bill." When you are enjoying the fresh taste of your favorite food, take a moment to be grateful. If you find yourself reveling in the feel of a breeze on your cheek, be grateful for your ability to feel that exquisite sensation.

- Practice having each person around the dinner table express a gratitude. Children love doing this with friends and family!

One of my teachers, Pema Chödrön, wrote that she is grateful for the really tough times in her life because it has allowed her to connect compassionately with other sufferers.

- See if you can find lessons for your growth in a challenging situation. What qualities is the difficult time demanding that you develop? Patience? The ability to surrender to what is? Determination? Focus?

Notice how deepening your gratitude practice affects the quality of your life.

Here's an example of unexpected gratitude:

Susan's Story

I once had an experience with gratitude that shook me to my core. It was over thirty years ago and I was feeding my infant daughter carrots.

Bright orange mushy carrots covered her face, my arms, and the tray of her highchair. Suddenly, as though a veil had dropped, I felt overwhelming, bone-deep, all-encompassing gratitude that I was able to feed my child nourishing food. It wasn't a thought—it was totally unexpected and outside the range of my ordinary experience. I've never had a similar experience of gratitude, but that one has kept me faithful to my own Gratitude Practice.

You now have a Resource Inventory that you can review, add to, and use to remind yourself of the rich mix of qualities, characteristics, interests, talents, and appreciations with which you can support your resilience and well-being. You've created your Resource Reminder to quickly remind yourself of your unique brilliance. Your daily Gratitude Practice will nourish your heart and soul.

Use these and you'll naturally become more confident, appreciative, lively, and light-hearted.

CHAPTER 5: TAKE YOUR BEST FRIEND WITH YOU

"Friendship is a sheltering tree." *~Samuel Taylor Coleridge*

Like many people, you may not be aware of the almost constant chatter of judgments, associations, compressed imagery, and commentary that goes on in your mind. You may think of it as a low-grade background noise and, unless you tune into it, you'll have no idea of the impact it has on your sense of self. Often, especially when they're annoyed with themselves, people say things internally that they wouldn't dream of saying to another person.

Talking harshly to yourself is the equivalent of expecting yourself to walk gracefully while at the same time hitting your own toes with a hammer. It doesn't work. The impact is the opposite of creating the peace of mind you long for. Critical inner self-talk inhibits growth, dries up creativity, and blocks openness and self-trust.

Now is the time for you to start creating inner safety and calm by developing a matter-of-fact and non-judgmental attitude toward your inner chatter as a step toward learning to filter out harsh and unfriendly talk and attitudes.

More of Joan's Story

> *I asked Joan, whom you met in Chapter 4, to tune into her inner dialogue to notice both what she was saying to herself and how she felt in her body when she noticed what she was saying.*
>
> *To start, Joan judged her self-talk as "stupid." I reminded her that she was practicing non-judgmental self-observation and encouraged her to begin this process with her interested and curious attitude. Joan was about to learn a core skill that would help her greatly as she moved toward her goal of learning to enjoy her life more.*
>
> *To heighten her awareness of the impact of her inner voice, I asked Joan to tell me how she talked to herself when she was annoyed with herself. She started off hesitantly but warmed up when I encouraged her to use the tone of voice she used on herself. It was a contemptuous voice.*

"I can never get it right!" "I never do enough." "No matter how well I do, I feel stupid." "I should do better." "What's wrong with me?"

Joan recognized the words as ones she'd used on herself as a child in her family home in response to her parent's academic expectations. She'd continued to berate herself over her presumed flaws for many years.

Joan reported that she felt constricted in her chest and as though there was a band around her neck as she repeated those familiar words.

I thanked Joan for sharing her inner critical voice and then encouraged her to come back to the present, to "come back into the room" and attend to her buildup of tension. Joan anchored on her breath, breathed into the areas of tightness in her chest and neck, and used her exhalations as an opportunity to soften and release tension. She increased her awareness of her feet on the ground, her weight in the chair, the quality of air in the room, and the fact that she and I were in the room together. When Joan did this, she said she could feel her tension dissolving.

I then asked her if she would be willing to do an exercise using the familiar contemptuous words she had spoken. Joan agreed.

Open-Door Closed-Door Exercise

I asked Joan to imagine the following: "The door to my counselling office opens. A woman enters the room who looks as though she could be your twin. You know intuitively that the quality of the rest of your life depends on the relationship you have with this woman. She sits down and looks at you as though she wants to get to know you. You turn to her and say in the scornful tone you use on yourself, 'You can never get it right! And you never do enough! And no matter how hard you try, you come off stupid! You can do better! What's wrong with you?'"

I then asked Joan what she thought the woman would say to her. Joan didn't answer me. I said, "I think she'd say, 'I'd hoped we could get to know each other but that's not going to happen if you're going to talk to me like that.' Then she'd get up and leave the room, closing the door behind her."

Joan looked thoughtful and agreed.

Joan's words affect her inner life even more strongly than they would the imaginary stranger or any other person in her life. Joan really got it. She said that she had found the exercise "really powerful." She was now ready to carry on and learn to use the Friendship Filter.

Other people can walk away from you if you treat them poorly. You can't walk away from yourself. Of course, there are many ways you can abandon yourself, for example, with addictions, by creating drama distractions, or by shutting down, but you can never walk away from the results of what you do to yourself. You are stuck with yourself.

You learn disrespectful self-talk early, sometimes unintentionally and subtly, other times very bluntly, from your caregivers, your families, your peers, and teachers, song lyrics, movies—the whole cultural smorgasbord. Put-downs can feel familiar and oddly right.

In addition, children often believe that they are responsible for family upsets—that it's their fault if a parent is in distress, or that they should be able to keep the family together. They often carry these beliefs into adulthood, unconsciously. If this has been your experience, you can carry on without being aware of the beliefs but feeling their impact—low self-esteem, shame, anxiety, a whole host of painful feelings.

By beating yourself up internally, you inadvertently create what you don't want for yourself. For example, saying "I don't deserve what I want!" to yourself over and over reinforces a feeling of unworthiness. Remember not to beat yourself up for beating yourself up! If you start getting caught in that loop, just notice that it's happening, and actively switch your focus. Stretch, move your body. Drink some water. Go gently with yourself, especially if this kind of self-observation is new for you.

EXERCISE 5.1 Develop and Use a Friendship Filter

Give yourself an hour of uninterrupted time.

You'll need your writing materials for these exercises.

Before you start, settle in by anchoring on your breath, feeling your weight on the chair, and your feet on the floor.

Step 1: Notice

- Begin by tuning in to your inner dialogue. Imagine you have a dial on that background sound and you are going to turn it up to tune in. Initially, don't try to change what you notice. Just notice.

Our mind produces thoughts. Sometimes it offers a flash of an image that may evoke a whole cluster of feelings; sometimes it's snippets of songs we heard on the radio. Our thoughts are often generated by subtle or attention-focusing shifts in our physical sensations—such as a faster heartbeat or clenching in our gut. Just notice. Don't expect anything in particular.

Step 2: The Three Friendship Filter Questions

Once you have taken some time to kindly and non-judgmentally observe your inner dialogue and accompanying sensations, start to filter out any put-downs you may notice by asking yourself the following three Friendship Filter questions:

1. Would I say that to anybody else in the world?

2. Would I say that to a good friend?

3. Would I say that to someone with whom I wanted to develop a lifelong, loving relationship?

If the answer to any of those questions is "No," don't say it to yourself!

When you do notice that you're saying something disrespectful and unkind to yourself, something you wouldn't say to a good friend, beloved child, or lifelong lover, label it by naming it something like 'negative self-talk', 'put down', 'mean girl', 'inner bully', or whatever descriptive term works for you and counter it energetically, then shift your focus.

An exercise that clearly demonstrates how to do this follows.

Sometimes that critical voice is so familiar it feels like just the way things are. It is not the way things are. That critical voice is an old, disrespectful learned habit and has nothing to do with your inherent worth.

Physical feedback will give you clues as to how you are talking to yourself. If you notice yourself getting tense, feeling disappointed or droopy, check your self-talk for put downs. For example, if you are at a public event and start to feel uneasy, check to see if you're comparing yourself unfavorably to someone else; or if you have just criticized yourself for a comment you just made.

Step 3: Recognizing and Countering Your Disrespectful Inner Voice

Remember a time when you were fed up or disappointed with yourself. Maybe it took you six times to learn something that you thought you should have picked up in two and you feel impatient with yourself. Perhaps you drove your new car over a barrier in the parking lot right in front of the colleague who is so critical and you felt humiliated. Maybe you forgot a good friend's birthday and felt guilty. Maybe you were edgy with your dying friend and felt ashamed of yourself.

- Remember now how you spoke to yourself when you were upset with yourself. Use the tone of voice you used on yourself. Jot down three to five things you say to yourself in your most impatient, discouraged, harsh, or scolding tone.

If you are thinking "Well actually, I treat myself well, this doesn't apply to me." That's good. Just for interest's sake give this exercise a try anyway.

Take a moment now to shake out any tension that may have built up while doing this exercise before continuing.

Take three tension-reducing breaths.

Look around the room. Focus on a color or shape that you enjoy.

Refocus on this exercise.

Step 4: Speak Kindly to Yourself

- Say clearly to yourself, "Those are examples of my inner insulter. It's not okay for me to talk to myself like that. Never was and never will be. I'm learning to filter out that hurtful talk. I'm using my Friendship Filter."

- Then think of what you would say to a friend who was equivalently self-critical in each of those circumstances and write that down. Offer yourself the same quality of kindness and respect that you would a dear friend.

Step 5: Release Tension

- Use one of the BFTR techniques to shift your body

from tension and constriction to a more expansive, comfortable, and relaxed state.

Again, if you wouldn't say it to a friend, don't say it to yourself. This is important.

This isn't about having no expectations of your own behavior or supporting a lack of inner discipline. In fact, it takes inner discipline to do this work. You can be firm and kind. If you are fed up with something—for example, your lack of exercise—rather than calling yourself a "disgusting, lazy slob," say, "Oops, inner insulter." (naming the put-down language) "Learning to treat myself with respect. Sorry, self. Forgive me. It's time to go to the gym, even if you don't feel like it!" Or if you're not quite ready to go to the gym, you might say, "Sorry for talking to you that way, self. Forgive me. I'd prefer to be more active." Or, "Time to treat myself with respect just the way I am."

Experiment with using different pronouns, (I, we, they, or you) when you talk to yourself to see which you find most engaging. Further explanation of the use of pronouns follows in Exercise 5.2.

From now on, direct your self-talk through a Friendship Filter.

Your inner atmosphere will start to shift over time as you consistently do this. Your old critical comments will come to feel increasingly unfamiliar and as though they don't belong or relate to you. This will take persistent practice.

Notice what comes up for you as you transition to living with a safer, kinder, gentler inner climate. You may find yourself feeling uncomfortable without the familiar inner critical voice. Use your breath to release tension and remind yourself that you're learning new ways. Notice, as your new sense of inner safety develops, how it affects your relationships with others. Notice any physical shifts you may have as you treat yourself with kindness and compassion.

Every now and again someone I work with finds it hard to imagine using a Friendship Filter. If that is the case for you, start by practicing imagining what it will be like to talk to yourself matter-of-factly. Gradually shift in the direction of speaking to yourself kindly and respectfully.

The idea of the Friendship Filter is that eventually, when you travel alone or go home alone and shut the door, rather than being with an indifferent, undermining, or hostile stranger, you're with a friend you can trust, a friend you can count on to treat you well, who will appreciate you and acknowledge your value and worth. Someone you can have fun with. Self to self. And no, this isn't being self-absorbed and selfish. It's learning to treat yourself as respectfully as you treat others.

It's offering your best self, your generosity, and your compassion to yourself as well as to others.

Think about a time you fell in love. Did you think that this was finally the sweetheart, the soulmate who would accept and cherish you just as you are? What if it turns out that you are the one you have been waiting for? What if it is you who gets to accept yourself just as you are, be true to yourself, love yourself, be trustworthy and faithful—in sickness and in health?

You'll notice that as you move in the direction of developing a respectful, acknowledging, more loving, and compassionate inner relationship, you'll meet the people in your life with a generous overflow of the good feelings you have generated internally. As well, you'll have less tolerance for disrespectful behavior from others.

- Take a moment now to sit with what you've learned.

- Sense the difference using the Friendship Filter can make to the quality of your life.

- Smile to yourself.

Shift and stretch. Take a short break.

Carry on to the next exercise.

EXERCISE 5.2 Develop and Use Your Inner Coach

Your Inner Coach is a close relative to your Inner Friend. The job of your Inner Coach is to offer you encouragement in the world and give you caring guidance, backing, and support.

An example might be:

You didn't get the job you wanted and thought you had done a great interview. Your Observer Self notices, in a matter-of-fact, non-judgmental way, "Disappointment, shame, self-blame." As your Inner Coach, you might say kindly to yourself, "You're really disappointed. No need for blame or shame. Well done for going for it! Keep at it; you're getting better all the time. Tomorrow maybe you could call Tony and get some coaching on interview techniques. You can review this whole thing then. Breathe and release tension. That's it. You're doing fine; how about a cup of tea and then a run?"

If you are wondering why I suggest you speak to yourself in the second person as in 'You are disappointed,' rather than in the first person as in 'I am disappointed,' it's to support you in developing a slightly detached observer stance toward your inner processes. This allows you to feel your feelings and body sensations fully while at the same time observing them in a kind, matter-of-fact, accepting way. If you feel uncomfortable using the second person use 'I' or 'we.'

If you are a mom or dad with a young child, you may be skilled at coaching already. You can transfer your coaching skills so that you benefit from your own active encouragement.

Step 1: Remember

- Think of three recent times when you found yourself

in situations where you felt anxious, unappreciated, or upset.

- Jot down brief descriptions of each of those challenging times.

Step 2: Release Tension

- Refocus on your current surroundings and anchor on your breath.

- Practice releasing any buildup of tension you may observe using a BFTR technique.

Step 3: Describe Your Inner Coach

Now think about your ideal Inner Coach. This could be an imaginary person, a respected elder, a public figure you admire, your guardian angel, your own wise self, a special friend—whatever feels right for you.

- Write a description of your ideal Inner Coach

Step 4: Replay the Situations

- In your imagination, replay the three situations you thought of in Step 1 of this exercise, one at a time. This time imagine that your ideal Inner Coach is right there with you, coaching you through each of those difficult situations as your inner voice of mentoring support.

Step 5: Create an Encouraging Script

- Write down as a script what your Inner Coach would say to you in each of those tough situations. Use a kind, caring, matter-of-fact tone with yourself.

- Use your breath to release tension.

Step 6: Use Your New Coaching Script

- Use those encouraging words and scripts to support yourself the next time you are in similar situations.

You can use your Inner Coach to support yourself through an uncomfortable event as it's happening or later when you review the situation to learn from it.

Review to learn rather than to self-recriminate, then let the situation go—release it. You can reinforce the letting go physically by firmly brushing imaginary flour off your hands.

Take a few deep breaths. Have a glass of water. Look out a window. Refresh yourself.

EXERCISE 5.3 Develop and Use Your Inner Ideal Parent

Few of us grow up with our ideal parents. Parents usually try hard to do their best, and at times are good-enough parents, occasionally even good or great parents. However, for a variety of reasons such as illness, addiction, stress, inadequate parenting skills, family crisis, or money issues, there can be many times when a parent's caregiving is inadequate for the needs of their children. Because children are dependent on their early caregivers for survival, parent-child interactions can carry a reactive, life-or-death flavor into adulthood.

Part of taking charge of your inner life is to take over the role of parenting yourself by developing and using the voice and attitude of your Inner Ideal Parent.

You may be thinking, "I'm so past that. I've been on my own for years." People on their deathbeds in their nineties have been known to call for their mothers. Unprocessed pain from early years can fester a lifetime and be passed down through generations.

Step 1: Remembering for Review and Revision

- Remind yourself of your Resource Statement. You are in a very different stage of your life than you were as a vulnerable child.

- Now, review different periods of your life focusing on the parenting you received.

- Take a tension-releasing breath.

- Write down three times when you wanted or needed a different kind of parenting than you received.

Step 2: Release Tension

- Take a deep, slow breath in; slowly release it fully on your exhalation. Do this three times. Remind yourself: "That was then (each of the circumstances you just wrote about) and this is now."

- Look around at your surroundings. Feel your feet on the floor, your weight in the chair. Remind yourself again that you are now an adult and your current circumstances are very different than they were when you were a child.

Step 3: Imagine Your Ideal Parents

- Think about examples of positive parenting you have witnessed or read about.

- Remind yourself that very few of us have had ideal parents.

- Imagine who your ideal parents would have been when you were younger. You could choose a neighbor, a friend's parents, or a family member. You could choose your actual parents or earlier caregivers if they had offered the love, care, support, and guidance you wanted and needed. You could choose a beloved character taken from books or movies. You could model them on famous people living or dead.

You may feel disloyal to your parents or early caregivers, (who more than likely did the best they could) when you think of creating your ideal inner parents. Remind yourself, this is not to disrespect your parents or caregivers, but rather to acknowledge the impact their parenting had on you as a child. It is now time for you to take over the parenting role for yourself. Wish them well and know that you, and they, will benefit from this practice. Return to the exercise.

Step 4: Create Inner Ideal Parent Scripts

Imagine what your ideal parents would have done or said in each of the three instances you chose in Step 1. If you are uncertain about what an ideal parent would say, imagine a kind, interested, loving person with whom you feel safe and cared for attending to you in a way that you feel totally acknowledged and accepted.

- Create and write out Inner Ideal Parent scripts for yourself for each of those three situations.

- How would you have felt receiving their nurturing attention? What do you notice in your body as you think about this? What other feelings come up for you? Just notice with compassion. Let your feelings move through you without attaching old stories to them.

- Remember to breathe and keep your fingers and toes soft and relaxed as you do this exercise.

Step 5: Be Your Own Ideal Parent

If you notice that you are inwardly cringing because you are giving yourself criticisms or judgments that you know come from your early internalized parents—stop.

- Remind yourself that you are taking over the parent role in your life. You can say to your internalized parent voices from the past, "Thank you for everything you did to support and care for me. I never needed and don't need your criticism and judgments (or whatever characteristics or behavior you are releasing), I am taking over now!"

- Replace the disrespectful, learned inner talk with your ideal parent scripts. How would your ideal mother or father acknowledge you, guide you, support you, celebrate you?

- Practice talking to yourself with the compassion, interest, and support of your ideal inner parents.

Notice any shifts in your attitude toward your actual parents (or early caregivers), alive or not, as you take full responsibility for your inner parenting. You may notice that you start to see them as vulnerable, flawed human beings. You may feel compassion for them. Remember to offer yourself compassion too. You were very vulnerable as a child and could not have known then what you know now.

Acknowledge yourself for giving yourself the gift of learning to use your Friendship Filter, Inner Coach, and Inner Ideal Parents. Eventually, these can merge into one kind, compassionate, and matter-of-fact inner voice. For now, use these tools consistently to release self-criticism and to become genuinely self-accepting. Your confidence will grow.

You may notice yourself having more fun, becoming livelier, and feeling more creative and spontaneous as you journey on—now that you can count on your inside support.

Chapter 6: Fascinating Stories

"There is no reality except the one contained within us." *~Hermann Hesse*

One of the main ways we maintain our sense of self is through the stories we tell ourselves over and over, day in and day out about who we are and what we can expect of ourselves, others, and the world. We develop these stories—about our worth, abilities, vulnerabilities, and possibilities—early on as we experience the societies we are born into through our families, schools, communities, the media. Often our storylines are outdated leftovers from our families and may have been passed down through the generations.

These stories feel true and real because they become entrenched in our bodyminds and form the lens through which we make sense of our world.

We get confirmation and reinforcement of the way we view the world because we filter our experiences selectively, literally not seeing what doesn't fit our beliefs about the way things are. Plus, when people are emotionally invested in their beliefs, "factual information to the contrary only makes them cling to their beliefs more tenaciously." (Nyhan, B and Reifler J., *When Corrections Fail, Political Behavior,* 2010). That sentence is worth repeating and remembering in the heat of an argument!

A study called *The Invisible Gorilla Test: On the Phenomenon of Inattention Blindness* (Chabris, C., and Simons, D., Harvard University, 2004) inspired the creation of a video in which six people, half wearing white shirts and half black, were filmed playing basketball. People watching the video in the study were asked to keep silent count of the number of passes players in the white shirts made. During the game, a gorilla walked past the players, looked at the camera, thumped its costumed chest, and then walked off camera. Only half of the people watching the video and counting passes saw it. For the other people, the gorilla didn't exist. If you don't expect to see something, it is likely you won't see it. To my chagrin, I did not see the gorilla the first time I saw the video. I was busy counting passes by white-shirted players.

Not only do people cling to distorted versions of what is and fail to include evidence available to their own eyes—their habitual behavior often influences other people and circumstances to confirm for them that their view of the world is correct. In this way, our stories create the self-fulfilling lens through which we filter our experiences. For example, the person who is taught that the world is a threatening and fearful place, or who believes that they are not smart enough to make their own way will have a very different experience than someone who believes that they are capable and resilient, and that the world is abundant with opportunity and possibility.

Sarah's Story

Sarah came to counselling because she was feeling painfully isolated. She came from a family culture that gave her the message, "There can never be enough..." (of love or material goods or pleasure). She accepted this family story as truth and didn't notice the opportunities, appreciation, and affection that did come her way. What she did notice was that these approaches made her feel uncomfortable and awkward as they didn't fit her belief about what was possible for her. She actively pushed them away. Eventually, the people around Sarah stopped offering or asking because of her lack of responsiveness and what they felt as her prickliness.

Not only did Sarah unwittingly prove what she learned in her family, she also assumed that the people around her thought she was unworthy or undeserving, or that she wanted too much. She assumed they believed what she regarded as truth about herself and didn't understand that they were reacting to her own presentation. Sarah had proved to herself that it was inevitable that she would always miss out.

Here is an example of a person blind to his present because he believes his old limiting story:

Jeffrey's Story

Even though he'd had several relationships, because of his early experiences of rejection, Jeffrey believed it was his lot to be alone in life. He planned to leave his relationship with Evelyn (thus finding himself alone again) before she left him after an argument, so that he didn't have to experience the pain of Evelyn inevitably leaving him (this was Jeffrey's story).

Evelyn's truth was that she wanted Jeffrey to stay and work things out with her.

In these ways, we prove to ourselves that what we believe is true.

When you're reminded of something that happened in the past, you may find yourself responding viscerally with reactions that may have been appropriate for that earlier event but that are out of sync, exaggerated or that appear irrelevant or irrational and unrelated to present circumstance. If this happens, you have an opportunity to become aware of your underlying beliefs as well as your repetitive self-talk and default emotional reactions that help hold them in place. These out-of-context reactions are called triggered reactions.

There are ways to disempower and unhook from the stories that hem you in and anchor you to outdated beliefs. With your matter-of-fact Observer Self, you can notice if you're feeling triggered. You can observe yourself storytelling and name those old stories for what they are: obsolete, unnecessary, and limiting. You can bring yourself back to the present. You can ask yourself, "Does this belief—or assumption, feeling, thought, or action—lead me in the direction of the flourishing life I want for myself?" "Is it supporting my peace of mind?" "Am I willing to challenge my old stories?" "Am I willing to open up to new attitudes and beliefs?" "Am I willing to support my well-being?" "Is this attitude congruent with the person I am choosing to become?" Or you can simply notice and name it "old, outdated story" and refocus on the present.

Your Observer Self is your meta-observer. It's an internal aspect that notices (and can name) the comings and goings of your inner life—not only your old repetitive stories, but

also your thoughts and feelings, sensations, energy levels, emotions, moods, and daydreams—all with non-reactive acceptance. It's helpful to think of the Observer Self as a kind, matter-of-fact overseeing inner aspect that provides a way for you to observe your inner processes without becoming reactive to them.

Sometimes people worry that if they identify with an Observer Self, their feelings won't be as real or vivid, or that they will have to shut down their feelings. The reverse is true. With practice, using your Observer Self creates a sense of inner spaciousness that will allow you to observe your feelings come and go and experience them fully without shutting down or feeling overwhelmed by them.

If you do notice yourself becoming reactive or feeling overwhelmed, using the Observer Self can help you identify choice points where you can intervene to support yourself with your BFTR practices and your Friendship Filter, Inner Coach, or Ideal Parent. This will take patience and practice and is worth the effort.

Here's an example of how using the Observer Self helped Alecia as she went through an unwanted breakup with the man she loved

Alecia's Story

Three years before Alecia came for counselling, she met Jeremy in Thailand when they were

both on vacation. It turned out that they were both from Vancouver. For Alecia, it was love at first sight. She had never felt such powerful feelings of magnetic attraction to another person. Jeremy said he felt the same. Three months after returning home, they moved in together and enjoyed two blissful years.

Following his parents' death in an automobile accident, Jeremy began to withdraw from Alecia. By the time she insisted on couples counselling, Jeremy told Alecia that the relationship was over. Alecia was devastated and felt the most intense feelings of loss and sadness she had ever known. She felt as though she was drowning. The devastating story she told herself was, "I'll never fall in love again. No one will ever love me again. I'm going to be alone forever." She was miserable.

In counselling, Alecia wept and said she could hardly bear her pain. Gradually she learned to tolerate the intensity of her emotions, to soothe and compassionately hold herself. She began to practice using her Observer Self to watch the rising and falling of her strong feelings. In doing this, she gradually developed enough internal spaciousness to tolerate her experience of grief and loss without feeling as though she would disintegrate every time a fresh wave threatened to engulf her. She began to notice how her thoughts and feelings affected each other. She used the BFTR techniques to help herself physically and emotionally soften to her pain. She began to allow herself to be comforted by the support of her friends and family.

Alecia also learned to coach herself through the waves of her intense feelings: "I can make it through this one breath at a time." "I can grow my tolerance for this grief." "This is a hard enough time; I don't have to make it worse by telling myself scary stories like I'm going to be alone forever." She was learning to ride the waves of her emotional life as they came and went, using BFTR techniques, her Observer Self, Friendship Filter, and Inner Coach. After six counseling sessions, Alecia reported that while this was the toughest time she had lived through, she had moments of enjoying herself when she was with her friends and that she was feeling more hopeful about her future.

Here is an example of how Sam's story changed as he realigned himself in the direction of his goal of reclaiming a sense of internal peace and stability.

Sam's Story

Sam is a stocky single man in his mid-fifties. After graduating from college, he joined the public service and worked hard to achieve his status as a middle manager. He liked his co-workers and felt that his contributions were valued by his boss, Wendy, who had hired and mentored him.

Sam was thrown into internal turmoil when Wendy left and was replaced by Sarah, a bright, degreed woman fifteen years his junior. Sarah made some structural changes that only peripherally impacted him, but Sam was very anxious about the changes and convinced himself that Sarah wanted to get rid of him. That was his story. On his weekends, he obsessed over what was going on at the office. He kept himself awake at night worrying and reviewing details of conversations he'd had with Sarah. He gossiped about her with his co-workers. He came to counselling because he felt stressed and wanted to regain his sense of inner peace.

Sam had his goal. I encouraged him to develop his Resource Inventory. In doing this, he reminded himself of his competency and skills at work and the respect his former boss and his co-workers gave him. This helped him feel on more solid ground than he had for months. Sam was shifting his story. I encouraged him to engage in enjoyable activities that had nothing to do with work. He decided that he would sign up for a Spanish class. Sam had become very self-critical and was a tough internal taskmaster, much more than he was with the people who reported to him. He adopted the Friendship Filter which gave him a guideline for treating himself more respectfully. Sam agreed that gossiping with his co-workers about Sarah only fueled his anxiety, increased his stress, and drained his energy. It was a block to finding out what the potential was for them to develop a satisfying working relationship.

After a slow start, Sam developed his ability to self-monitor using his kind, non-judgmental Observer Self. He began to notice when he was tempted to go to his co-worker to get the goods on office gossip and refocused by asking himself if doing that would take him toward or away from his goal of inner peace and stability. He used the same strategy when he caught himself scaring himself with "what ifs" about his future work life.

Sam's self-respect grew as he learned to manage his inner life and, in the process, create a new narrative of possibility for himself.

EXERCISE 6.1 Using Your Accepting, Non-Reactive Observer Self

Practice using the Observer Self to notice your thoughts, feelings, sensations, and familiar default emotional states as they come and go.

This exercise will take about twenty minutes.

You'll need privacy, quiet, and focused attention.

Make sure you're comfortably seated with your feet on the floor and your spine straight.

Bring yourself present by taking three complete Breath Focusing-Tension Releasing breaths.

After you've read through or listened to this exercise, sit in a relaxed yet alert posture while you practice developing a compassionate, accepting, matter-of-fact Observer Self.

If you find yourself becoming uncomfortable or anxious closing your eyes or focusing this way—stop. This simply means that this exercise is not for you. Carry on by choosing exercises that you find more helpful.

Step 1: Just Notice

- Begin by focusing on your breath. Attend to the sensations of your inhalation and exhalation as they enter and leave your body—easily, no forcing. This is called "anchoring on the breath." Do this for several breaths. Then expand your focus to include observing how your lungs and belly expand and contract as you inhale and exhale. Imagine that you're gently taking your breath *in the direction of* behind and just below your navel.

- When you find yourself becoming distracted—perhaps by your reaction to a sound, or by thinking about your next meal, feeling irritated, planning a grocery list, fantasizing about sex, or worrying about rent money—just notice this without judgment and patiently, kindly and firmly refocus your attention on your breath. Anchor on your breath. Begin again. You're learning to observe your inner life with acceptance, without telling yourself stories about what you notice. You are aiming in the direction of accepting, non-reactive self-observation.

- You may notice that you've become lost in elaborating on an old story or fantasy—name it. For example, you might notice and name "old worrying story," "fantasizing," "irritation story," "familiar angry thoughts," "old embarrassing memory," and so on. After you have done that, simply go back to anchoring on your breath and then to your patient attention to your inhalation and exhalation.

- If you become distracted by a physical sensation, maybe your nose starting to itch, or a familiar pain, notice this without judgment, scratch the itch, shift your posture, and refocus on your breath. Begin again.

A daily ten to twenty-minute practice of this quiet, non-reactive, accepting self-observation can shift the quality of your life. With regular practice, you can create the foundation for a calm, kind, and matter-of-fact approach to your inevitably changing inner and outer circumstances.

Step 2: With Interest and Curiosity

Observe how your thoughts are affected by your range of physical sensations, such as tension, pain, constriction, pleasure, or expansion.

- How are your thoughts affected by slowing and

deepening your breathing?

- How does a default emotional state, such as disappointment, defeat, or irritation affect the quality of your thoughts and how you experience your body?

- What's it like to observe and experience your more immediate, fluid feelings come and go without reacting to them?

- Tune in to your thoughts, emotional states, feelings, and body sensations at different times throughout your day. Be particularly alert to times when you notice yourself reacting to events in your inner or outer life. Ask yourself what a response would be that's in alignment with your deeply held values.

Here is an example of a woman using her Observer Self to interrupt a familiar pattern of anxiety by engaging her Friendship Filter and Inner Coach:

Sue's Story

Sue was cooking when she thought, "What if George gets in a traffic accident on the way home for dinner?" She had a sinking feeling in the pit of her stomach. With her matter-of-fact Observer Self, she named that thought "scary thought," and the sensation "sinking feeling in my stomach." She reminded herself, "I'm learning not to scare myself. Sorry, self, forgive me." She placed her left hand over her heart in a comforting gesture. She took a moment to become aware of her physical surroundings, the feeling of the air on her skin, her weight on her feet, the sensations of the dishcloth in her right hand. She then took three focused tension-releasing breaths. Sue supported herself with a reality-based reassuring coaching comment. "If there were trouble, I'd get a call. There hasn't been a call. I'm learning to assume that things are going to be okay rather than assuming the worst." She then refocused on making dinner.

Another example:

Vic's Story

Vic had a deadline looming. He had a habit of daydreaming and losing his focus. He noticed with his Observer Self that he was daydreaming. Vic named what he was doing, "fantasizing." He reminded himself, "I'm learning to stay present so that I can meet my deadline." He took a moment to become aware of his surroundings and his inner sensations. He drank some water, took a tension-releasing breath, and refocused on his project.

Your Observer Self illuminates the countless choice points for transformation available to you—opportunities to release your reactivity, your outdated stories, habits and accompanying tension. You can choose to develop new, healthy habits and bring yourself more present. You can make your choices based on your up-to-date values and your intention to support your well-being—choice by choice.

Chapter 7: Supporting the Wisdom Body

"There is more wisdom in your body than in your deepest philosophy." *~Friedrich Nietzsche*

Many North Americans have an ambivalent, indifferent, if not contemptuous relationship with some part, or all, of their bodies. Both men and women are often deeply distrustful or ashamed of their bodies, believing that the body betrays them in illness, in the creases and folds of old age or by its often inconvenient and urgent demands. It's too often a "Shut up and do what I say" type of relationship. Knees that have been taken for granted on the soccer field and when running a marathon are viewed as shockingly unfaithful when they start to complain. A rounded belly is covered self-consciously. Aging arms are mocked as "chicken wings."

The body is seen as an object rather than as an expression of our life force.

Imagine that your body is a person. Think about how you talk to your body and what you expect of your body. Use your Friendship Filter to realign your relationship with your body if you find yourself treating your body with disinterest, harshness, or contempt. Practice befriending and appreciating your amazing one-and-only body. When you touch yourself, do so consciously. When you bathe, don't just scrub mindlessly. Wash yourself consciously, gently and compassionately. Pay attention to sensations. You experience your world through your eyes, ears, mouth, hands and skin. Value them.

You are a biochemical, electrical, energetic, vibrational being. Your body in all its complexity reflects the journeys you have taken. The cells, tissues, organs, and systems of your body hold memories of the experiences around which you shaped meaning and from which emerged your beliefs. You embody your history, personal and ancestral; your traumas; your chronically held emotional rigidities; your flexibility and your resilience. Emotional and energetic blocks and physical congestions are intertwined. Your cells and whatever it is that leaves when you die, that Great Animating Mystery, are merged as long as you live and breathe. That's a lot to respect.

Your body is designed to move. If you don't move you'll seize up, get stiff, lose your flexibility and muscle mass. You'll feel congested. There are many benefits to movement, including improved mood (exercise is an effective antidepressant) and better brain functioning. Some people run marathons, kayak rapids, and climb mountains. Fortunately, you don't have to be an athlete to benefit from moving your body!

Some people say they can't stand exercise or don't have the time to do it. Exercise can be as simple as a morning stretch or a series of joint rotations that you can do in just a few moments while you wait for the egg to boil. Here is a simple, short body wake-up routine.

EXERCISE 7.1 Body Wake Up Exercises

As a precaution check with a trusted professional to confirm that these exercises are suitable for you. If you already exercise regularly, you'll find Body Wake-up Exercises easy to incorporate into your routine, if they appeal to you.

When you're ready to do the exercises, make sure you have the privacy and space you need.

Take your time to practice each exercise and get comfortable with the routine suggested here.

If you can't stand, do as much as you can seated and then imagine yourself doing the rest of the exercises standing. Remember, your imagination is powerful!

These exercises are meant to be gentle. Please go at your own pace; don't overexert yourself. If you feel any pain or dizziness, please sit down, and take focused relaxing breaths. Adapt, adapt, adapt.

Wake up preparation:

When you first wake up and while you are still in bed, slowly and luxuriously stretch and greet your cells directly, sending them gratitude for all the work they do for you and visualizing them as healthy, glistening, refreshed and renewed. Your cells will respond with increased vitality to the inner atmosphere of well-being you create.

Do your morning gratitude practice.

Treat yourself to a refreshing glass of water.

Familiarize yourself with the entire Body Wake-Up routine by reading or listening from Step 1 to Step 4.

Step 1: Full-Breath Wake Up

When you are ready to start practicing the physical exercises:

- Take three gentle, deep breaths through your nose, imagining the air slowly filling your pelvic bowl. Soften and relax with each exhalation. Make your exhalations longer than your inhalations.

- Place your feet hip-width apart. Imagine that you are sending strong roots deep down into the earth. Lift your toes and place them back down, spreading them as evenly as you can. Feel your weight evenly distributed between your toes and heels and between your right and left feet.

- Hold your head gently upright, chin slightly tucked. Flex your knees slightly. Aim in the direction of feeling relaxed and alert.

In this exercise, you coordinate your arm movements with your breath to get a full inhalation and exhalation. Think of your inhalation as entering your lungs on a one-two-three count.

- On one, as you inhale through your nose, lift your arms in front of you until they are shoulder height, thumbs facing each other, palms down.

- On the two count of your same inhalation, take your arms straight out to your sides, shoulder height, hands palms down.

- On count three, lift your arms over your head, palms forward. You will have completed one full inhalation, no straining.

- Then, as you exhale in a whoosh through your mouth, bring your arms from above your head in a smooth movement down so that your thumbs are grazing the sides of your legs as you slightly bend your knees and bend your torso slightly forward. This is the classic about-to-ski-downhill posture and ends your exhalation. Adapt the exercise so that you enjoy the experience of doing it!

- That completes one inhalation/exhalation round. Straighten your knees until you are back to your original posture of having them slightly flexed.

Pause to check how you are feeling. One round may be enough to start. Take your time to work up to as many full-breath wake-up rounds as feel comfortable for you.

Step 2: Full-Joint Wake-Up

In this exercise, you rotate your joints, head to toe.

Neck: Turn your head to the left, moving in the direction of looking over your left shoulder. Then turn your head to the right, moving in the direction of looking over your right shoulder. Don't force this movement. If you can do it comfortably, repeat three times. Then, very gently and slowly rotate your neck in small circles. Imagine your nose is describing circles on a glass window in front of you. You can gradually increase the size of the circles you are drawing. Start with one or two gentle rotations in one direction, then reverse and do the same in the other direction. If it is comfortable for you to do so, over time you can build up to several rotations in each direction.

Shoulders: Now your shoulders. First, inhale and raise your arms above your head. Rotate forward and around with your outstretched arms in a full circle for two or three rotations as you exhale, then reverse direction. Inhale as your arms come up, and rotate backward, like a swimmer's butterfly backstroke, as you exhale. Again, start with a few rotations and increase the number of rotations and the speed at which you do them.

If it is difficult for you to rotate with your arms extended, do circles with your shoulders only, first forward, then back. If that is too painful, imagine yourself doing this part of the exercise.

Elbows: Hold your elbows loosely against your sides. Bend your arms to waist height and bring the tips of your fingers together over your abdomen. Describe circles with your lower arms by moving both hands in the direction of your knees, then to your sides, then up and around so that the fingertips brush again. Rotate first in one direction a few times, then the other. Gradually build up the number of rotations and to a speed that suits you.

Wrists: Rotate wrists, first in one direction and then the other. Again, gradually build up to a speed and number of rotations that feel right for you.

Hands: Now your hands. Hold your hands in front of you, palms up. Fold your thumbs toward the center of your palm. Fold your fingers over your thumbs. That is your starting position. Now simultaneously stretch the fingers of each hand up, one at a time, starting with the pinkies until all your fingers are extended. Extend the thumbs. Now both hands should be stretched open. Turn your hands over, fold in your thumbs, then one at a time fold in the rest of your fingers starting with your pointers and ending with the pinkies. Turn your hands over so the palms face up (starting position) and repeat the exercise. With practice this can become a graceful fan-like movement. Start by doing this one or two times and work up to more turns. This is an excellent exercise for maintaining finger joint flexibility.

Hips: In this exercise, protect your back by holding your abdomen firm, imagine your tailbone aiming in the direction of the ground beneath you, and never arch your back. Start with small rotations in as smooth a movement as you can manage, first moving your hips to the left, then tilting back, next tilting to your right, and finally tilting your pelvis forward. Make several rotations, first in one direction, and then the other. Check in with your body regularly to make sure you are not feeling discomfort or pain. If you are, stop. Listen to your body. If you are comfortable with the movements, you can make more expansive rotations. To help in making smooth hip rotations, visualize creating circles with your movement.

Ankles: Stabilize yourself by holding onto a wall or chair back. Shift your weight to your right foot, lift your left heel and rotate your left ankle, keeping your left big toe pivoting on the floor—first to the left, then to the right. Then shift your weight to your left foot, raise your right heel and rotate your right ankle, keeping your right big toe pivoting on the floor.

Complete this section by pausing, feet firmly planted, knees slightly bent, arms relaxed at your sides, to notice any inner shifts this simple series of movements has made.

Step 3: Invigorating Wake-Up Finger Tap

- Hold your fingers slightly apart and curved. With the fleshy part of the tips of your fingers, tap your scalp all over, vigorously, but not painfully.

- Tap along the top of your shoulders.

- Tap your upper chest and breastbone.

- Tap down each arm.

- Tap down each of your sides, starting a hand's width under each armpit.

- Tap down the sides of each of your legs twice, starting at your hips.

- Take a full breath or two and pause to experience the results of your finger tapping.

Step 4: Morning Wake-Up Series Completion

- Stretch your arms above your head in an open V and say, "Yes!" to your new day.

- With your arm up in the V, bend your elbows, bringing the tips of your middle fingers together, thumbs pointing toward your body. Sweep your hands down your body toward your feet. Imagine that you are smoothing out your energy as you prepare for your day.

- Return to your starting position, feet hip-width apart, knees slightly bent, hands relaxed by your sides, facing forward. Take two or three full, soft breaths. Feel yourself relaxed, alert and invigorated.

Enjoy how you feel. Appreciate the increased vitality you are bringing to your day as a result of having done this gentle practice.

End of Day Wind Down

Many people keep themselves awake at night obsessively reviewing events of the day or reminding themselves of all the things they have to get done the next day. You need your sleep to restore your bodymind. Your brain health depends on it. You reduce your ability to access your own intelligence, creativity and resilience if you don't meet your sleep needs. This greatly influences the quality of your presence at home and at work and shapes the life you create for yourself.

If you have difficulty falling asleep, experiment with unplugging from your electronic devices—all of them—a couple of hours before going to bed. Try having a warm bath or shower. Epsom salts in the bath a few times a week is a good detoxifier and essential oils can be soothing. Make your last meal of the day a light one. A sleepy-time herbal tea might help you settle as well.

If you know that your tendency is to lie there reviewing and analyzing, ask yourself if you're coming up with anything new and creative. If you aren't, stop and shift your attention. If you are busy making mental lists in the middle of the night, it may be time to get up, brew yourself a cup of non-caffeinated tea, sit down and write your plan for the next day. When you get back into bed and are tempted to make more lists, remind yourself that you've already done that and focus on your breath. Do the Breath Focusing-Tension Releasing technique, long form. Then shift your attention to the sensation of your sheets, the pillow under your head, and the weight of your body on the bed. Where do you feel pleasantly comfortable? Is there a breeze coming in through your bedroom window? Learning to do a full-body relaxation is an important basic skill to use when you want to drift off to sleep.

Your ideal bodymind default state before sleep is one of relaxed calm. In practicing this deep relaxation, you're familiarizing your bodymind with that preferred state.

EXERCISE 7.2 Full-Body Relaxation

Read through or listen to the full-body relaxation before starting. You may want to record this practice, so that you can fully focus on following the directions.

If you find yourself becoming anxious at any time while doing this practice, know that you can always open your eyes, bring yourself into present awareness, shift your focus and relax in a more familiar way. Sometime a not-very-interesting book is a perfect sleep inducer.

Step 1: Curious, interested attention

- If you have a painful or tense area that draws your attention, gently, kindly and firmly repeatedly redirect your attention to the area of relaxation focus. Incorporate this redirection into the relaxation practice.

- Start with three Breath Focusing-Tension Releasing breaths, Long Form. Allow yourself to settle in. Let the bed or chair support you.

Feet: On an inhalation, take your breath and your interested, curious attention into both your feet and explore the sensations in and around them. Explore and notice on your inhalation; relax and release on your exhalations. On your inhalations, you may notice itches, tingling, areas of pressure, sensations of fabric or leather, or feelings of heaviness or lightness. As you exhale, release, soften and imagine any holdings or tension flowing out of your relaxed toes, like a gentle current. On your inhalations, explore—you may not feel any sensations, just notice that—and soften and release on your exhalations. And one more inhalation to explore and exhalation to release. You are staying with your feet for three breaths.

Lower Legs: Take your focused attention and curiosity to your lower legs. As you inhale, explore—what do you notice between the bone and the skin? Do you notice any sensations? Can you feel air on your skin? The weight or pressure of clothing? As you exhale, let go, relax, and soften. Again, notice the sensations of your life in your calves on your next inhalation. Release, soften, and relax on your exhalation and imagine tension softly streaming down your lower legs, through your feet, and out of your toes. Stay with them for one more full breath.

Knees: Next, take your attention to your knees. As you inhale, what do you notice about those well-used hinge joints? Soften and release on your exhalation, imagining any holdings or tension running down your lower leg, through your feet, and out your toes. Inhale and notice sensations: pain, fabric stretched over your knees, the back of your knees—release and soften on your exhalation. One more time, explore on your inhalation; release on your exhalation.

Upper Legs: Take your focused attention to your upper legs. Feel your weight on the back of your legs. Explore with curiosity the space between the pressure of that contact and your leg bones on your inhalation. What do you notice? On your exhalation soften and release tension. On your next inhalation, feel your quadriceps from the outside in. Notice the weight of clothing or blankets on your upper legs. Soften and release tension on your exhalation. A third time, inhale and explore; exhale and soften, releasing tension.

Buttocks and Genitals: Take your curious attention to your buttocks and the whole area that is holding the majority of your weight if you're sitting. Explore with interest on your inhalation for any sensations of aliveness, pressure, numbness. As you exhale, soften, and imagine gentle currents of releasing tension flowing out of your body. Inhale, explore; exhale, soften, and release. And again inhale, explore; exhale and release.

Abdomen: Now begin to attend to your abdominal area with interest and curiosity on your inhalation. Imagine as you exhale and release that your inner organs relax deeper into the abdominal cavity as they let go of some of the tension they have been holding. Inhale and again explore this area where so many of us hold tension; release, soften, and imagine tension releasing—you could imagine it releasing directly out of your abdomen, or on your breath as you exhale. Make the exercise work for you. Again, inhale and explore; exhale, soften, and release.

Chest: Next, breathe into your chest cavity and as you breathe in to explore, imagine your breath supporting and soothing your heart and lungs so that as you exhale, they too can relax and soften. Again, take a soothing breath in as you explore your chest cavity, heart, and lungs with interested, relaxed attention, softening and letting go on your exhalation. One more inhalation, with curiosity; release and soften on your exhalation, letting tension leave on your out breath.

Spine: Now, on an inhalation, take your attention to the base of your spine. As you inhale, run your attention up either side of your spine. As you exhale, allow the muscles along either side of your spine to soften, release and relax so tension streams gently down your back, and into the earth. You are giving yourself a mini massage. Again, interested attention on your inhalation to the base of your spine and running focused attention up either side of your spine; on your exhalation, reversing direction and imagine held tension dissolving and streaming down your back and out of your body. And once more, explore on the inhalation and release on the exhalation.

Upper Back: Take your focused attention to your upper back. It's the area where so many people feel as though they are carrying the weight of the world on their shoulders. Take your soothing breath into that area, exploring your upper back and shoulders with interest and curiosity on your inhalation; releasing and softening on your exhalation. Imagine tension streaming down your arms and out your relaxed fingers. Explore with attention and curiosity on your inhalation; release and soften on your exhalation. If it works for you, imagine tension leaving your body on your breath, or simply evaporating out of your skin. And one more time, explore on the inhalation and release on the exhalation.

Arms and Hands: Go to your arms and hands as a unit. On inhalation, run your attention through your hands, lower arms, elbows, and upper arms, exploring for sensations—perhaps tightness, tingling, heaviness, lightness. As you exhale release, relax, and soften upper arms, elbows, lower arms, hands, and fingers. Imagine tension softly streaming down through your arms and out your fingers. Explore on your inhalations with focused curiosity, and soften and release tension on your exhalations for two more full breaths.

Neck: Now you are going to explore your neck on your inhalation. Slightly rotate your neck to focus your attention on that area. This is an amazing part of the body. So much information passes through it—every mental signal, every sensation—a constant flow of information back and forth. This is the area where you may hold yourself back from speaking, may choke back your truth or tears, or through which you sing your heart out. Explore on your inhalations; soften, release, and relax on your exhalations, imagining tension flowing gently out with your breath or streaming away as it flows down your body. Stay for two more rounds of inhalations and exhalations: exploring and releasing, exploring and releasing.

Face: Take your attention to your face. Most of us put energy into having a "publically acceptable" expression. This is your opportunity to allow gravity to hold you. Take your curious exploration into your facial muscles and release, relax, and soften with your exhalation. Imagine tension leaving on your breath. Let your eyes relax back into their sockets; allow your jaw to slacken. Breathe in, explore; breathe out, soften, and release. Breathe in, explore; breathe out, release.

Scalp: Take your attention to your scalp. This is another area where we hold tension. Imagine that you are breathing into your scalp and that with every exhalation your scalp relaxes a bit, releases tension, and softens over your skull. Inhale, explore; exhale, soften, and release, imagining tension softly streaming over your face and down your body like a gentle shower. Inhale, explore; exhale, soften, and release. One more time, inhale, explore; exhale, soften, and release.

Brain: Next take your attention to your brain, the organ (not your busy mind). With every inhalation imagine your breath soothing the brain as you explore for sensations; as you exhale, imagine your brain letting go of tension and relaxing back into the skull, settling back, tight folds softening. Breathe in, explore, notice whether or not you feel any sensations; exhale and imagine tension releasing through your breath. Inhale, explore; exhale, release. Inhale, explore; exhale, release.

Sweep: Take time now to imagine that a stream of effervescent energy originating at a spot just above your head is flowing over and through your body, gently sweeping your entire body clear of any remaining areas of tension.

Allow yourself time to marinate in this relaxed state.

Relaxing regularly is one of the kindest, most healing, and stress-reducing things you can do for yourself.

EXERCISE 7.3 Body Scanning

If you live only from the head up, you'll miss the constant streams of inside information that your body provides about the state of your well-being. Body Scanning is a way to tune into this information flow as you move through your day. As you practice this technique regularly, you'll become more conscious of your internal life. You'll recognize when you're engaged and enjoying yourself and when you're becoming reactive, stressed, or fearful. Combine Body Scanning with a Breath Focusing-Tension Releasing technique and your Inner Coach to support your relaxed alert state when you are out and about.

You will need fifteen minutes of uninterrupted time to read or listen to the following and practice the techniques.

Before you start the Body Scan, breathe in through your nose and imagine your breath gently and easily pouring down into your pelvis. Exhale slowly, either through your nose or mouth. Make your exhalation twice as long as your inhalation. Count to four on your inhalation and eight on your exhalation. See how that feels. If the exhalation is too long for you, switch to three or four on your inhalation and six on your exhalation.

Feel your weight in the chair and your feet on the floor.

Body Scanning Technique, Long Form

Step 1: Explore with focused attention, release tension

- Take your focused, interested attention through your body, scanning each of the areas described in the full body relaxation, feet to scalp, taking one full breath into each area. Explore on your inhalation and soften and release tension on your exhalation: feet, lower legs, knees, upper legs, buttocks and genitals, abdomen, chest, lungs, and heart; spine, upper back, arms and hands, neck, face, scalp, and brain. When you are releasing tension, visualize it leaving your body easily through your pores, on your breath, or streaming down your body.

- Reverse your direction. Explore, soften, and release through the areas from your scalp to your feet.

- If you notice holdings or discomfort, take a few more breaths into that area to soften and release tension on your exhalations. Imagine that you are bringing soothing, healing balm into those areas.

- Once you have done this, feel, or imagine, your healthy energy running smoothly throughout your body.

Body Scanning Technique, Short Form

Step 1: Explore more generally, with focused attention, release tension

- On an inhalation, combine exploration of your feet, lower legs, and knees. Exhale and release tension from those areas on your breath, soften. Inhale and explore your upper legs, buttocks, and genitals. Exhale and release tension, soften. Inhale and explore your abdomen, chest cavity—heart and lungs—and spine. Exhale and release tension, soften. Inhale and explore your upper back, upper and lower arms, hands, and fingers. Exhale, release tension, soften. Inhale and explore your neck, face, brain, and scalp. Exhale and release tension, imagining it streaming down your body.

- Reverse your direction of focus and repeat this process starting from your scalp.

- If you notice holdings or discomfort that need more attention to release, take a few more breaths into that area. Soften and release tension on each exhalation.

- As in the long form, imagine that you are bringing soothing, healing balm into those areas. Once you have done this, feel, or imagine, your healthy energy running smoothly throughout your body.

Body Scanning Technique, One Full Breath, The Wave

Step 1: One-Breath Full Body Scan: Inhale, Exhale, Release Tension

- On a long, slow inhalation, run your focused, interested attention through your entire body from your feet to your scalp. Hold your breath at the top of your head to the count of two. As you exhale, reverse direction, and imagine tension releasing and running down through your body from your scalp, out through the soles of your feet and your toes. Think of your breath rising and falling through your body as a rejuvenating wave.

- If you do find areas of tightness, pain, or tension, take additional soothing breaths into that area.

- Once you have done this, feel or imagine your healthy energy running smoothly throughout your body.

Body Scanning is an important skill to have in your relaxation repertoire. You can use Body Scanning during your busy day to spot-check yourself from the inside out to notice and release tension you may be carrying.

EXERCISE 7.4 Embodying Preferred States with Breath

An additional helpful use of breath is to breathe in a quality that you want to embody and release unwanted attributes on your exhalation. For example, if you want clarity, on your inhalation say silently to yourself, "Breathing in clarity." As you exhale, say silently to yourself, "Breathing out confusion, letting it go." At first, you may simply be breathing in a word, "clarity," and releasing a word, "confusion." As you continue this practice, you could imagine the quality of clarity (maybe the clarity of clean, fresh morning air) and breathe in that quality, imagining it suffusing every cell. Release confusion on your exhalation, perhaps visualizing it as fog that leaves on your breath or through your pores as you soften and exhale. Consciously shift your posture from the way you hold yourself physically when you are confused to the way you hold yourself when you experience clarity. When you do this, notice what happens to your breath.

For this exercise, you'll need a list of the values you decided are important to you (Chapter 3, EXERCISE 3.1, Step 2) and twenty minutes of uninterrupted time.

Read or listen to this entire exercise before you begin.

Center yourself by anchoring on your breath. Feel your feet connecting with the floor and your weight on the chair.

Step 1: Develop Qualities and Release Qualities

- Review your values. What inner qualities have you decided you'll develop in yourself to live your values fully? What qualities will you release?

Take your time to sink into this question for each of your values.

- Write down the qualities you committed to developing in yourself that embody your values (such as focus and determination) and what unhelpful habits or attributes (such as impatience and procrastination) you'll release.

- Beside each quality you want to embody, write a description of how you imagine you will hold yourself, what you'll think and feel, and how you'll behave differently when you own this quality.

- Do the same for the qualities you want to release. How will you think, feel and act differently without being burdened or hampered by each of those qualities?

Step 2: Use Your Powerful Imagination

- For each desired quality, practice breathing it in as an image, color, or felt sense on your inhalation.

- Release the unwanted quality as an image, color, or felt sense on your exhalation.

An example of the quality of courage could be breathing in the image of a golden lion heart of courage, and releasing fear as a cloud of swirling self-doubt on your exhalation.

- Experiment with imagery and words that work for you. When you inhale the quality you want to embody, imagine that quality surrounding, bathing, and entering your cells, and as you exhale, soften and release unwanted qualities on your breath or through your pores along with any holdings, constrictions, or tension that you notice.

A way to use breath embodiment when you're out and about is to notice when you appreciate something, such as the sun on your face. Take time to breathe in the sun's light and warmth, and to imagine the sun's energy saturating your cells. When you exhale, imagine releasing whatever may be blocking you from being fully present to receive the sun's energy.

Take time to appreciate yourself for engaging in these healing practices.

FOOD AS MEDICINE

A vital Wisdom Body practice is to support your well-being by eating a variety of nourishing, ideally organic, wholesome foods. Think of what you put in your body as medicine that supports your health, vitality, clarity, and enthusiasm for life. While there are diverse opinions about what constitutes healthy eating, most experts agree that fresh, non-processed foods are fundamental to any good plan. Do your research, experiment, and find what works for your unique circumstances, and precious one-and-only body.

Be kind to yourself, relax, and, whatever you decide is right for you, enjoy your food!

Regular use of your Wisdom Body practices will provide you with relaxation, vitality, and a grounded sense of well-being.

Congratulations on developing the well-integrated relationship with your bodymind that is fundamental to supporting your mental, emotional, and physical well-being, and your overall vibrant health. You are offering yourself a strong energetic foundation with which to meet your goals.

Chapter 8: Time Traveling

"Self-knowledge is only from moment to moment." ~ Krishnamurti

Most of us time travel—meaning we leave awareness of the present moment. We daydream about the past, enjoying how we believe things were, or longing for what was and is no more. We fantasize and we plan. We tell ourselves important stories about the way things were and the way things will be. While doing this, we're disconnected to some degree from our lives in the present. Nevertheless, out of this we create our lives, consciously or unwittingly. Sometimes we get lost in the fascinating stuff we make up. Other times we are jolted into time-traveling to a time when we felt vulnerable, unsafe, and unloved. We feel threatened by these feelings and react in habitual protective ways that are often detrimental to current relationships. In *Chapter 6: Fascinating Stories,* I called this phenomenon "being triggered." This is how we inadvertently sidetrack ourselves from being present and living our consciously stated values and goals.

The exercises in this chapter will give you tools to help you understand, navigate and repair any present reactivity you may have with understanding and compassion.

Here's a domestic example of a triggered response:

Donna and Marta's Story

Donna and Marta moved in together after dating for three years. They believed they knew each other well. They considered themselves to be great communicators. They had met with the approval of each other's families. For their entire courtship, Donna had been working part-time while she completed her Ph.D. thesis and had often been exhausted at the end of the day. Marta was settled in her work as a private consultant and had more energy than Donna, so she took over most of the cooking by mutual agreement.

One Saturday night shortly after they joined households, Donna told Marta that as a thank-you treat, she wanted to cook while Marta put up her feet. Marta liked this idea and settled in with her iPad. Donna happily went into what she called her "kitchen trance," humming tunelessly, chopping, dicing, and slicing. Marta smelled onions sizzling in the pan and wandered into the kitchen. "Why are you using grapeseed oil to stir fry the vegetables? Don't you think coconut oil would work better for the high temperature?" she asked, curious and interested. Donna looked up, startled. She straightened slowly, faced Marta, frowned, and said curtly, "Don't interfere like that. I'm cooking. Please get out of the kitchen!" Marta's eyebrows shot up, her jaw dropped and she stood looking in disbelief at her partner.

What happened?

Where did Donna's goodwill go? Why didn't she in a matter-of-fact way tell Marta, who is her best friend, her lover, and her partner, why she had made her choice? Or playfully remind Marta that she, Donna, was happily doing the cooking that evening and wanted the kitchen to herself to prepare a delicious meal—all questions answered at the table? Or get curious and have a discussion with Marta about the merits of various oils?

What happened was that Donna had time

traveled and had disconnected from her present-day partner, Marta. She was triggered and was reacting partly to unacknowledged feeling of vulnerability about setting up house with her partner. The strength of her reactivity, however, was fueled by experiences she had in her family of origin.

Donna was raised by a mother who often treated her as property, as though she were a pretty doll. Donna's mother could not conceive that Donna was an individual and saw her as an extension of herself. When Donna didn't conform to her mother's expectations, she was criticized severely, so she grew up silently conforming but inwardly resentful. When Donna left her family home, she carried within herself that seething child who had felt compelled to do things her mother's way. She now felt just as compelled to do things her own way. When Marta asked Donna about the oil, Donna had heard the question as criticism, as though her whole way of doing things—in fact, her whole being—was threatened. She reacted unconsciously to defend the threatened child she felt within.

Another example of triggered behavior, this time with Time Travel Repair work:

Mathew's Story

Mathew is an entrepreneur in the music business. With his colorful clothes, funky glasses, and jaunty walk, he looked like all was well in his world. He said he loved to travel and the adventure of high-risk sports. He talked rapidly and was uneasy with silence. Mathew came to counselling after a major upset with his girlfriend, Gynene. He loved Gynene, wanted to be with her, and had shocked himself with his strong feelings of outrage during an argument.

Mathew could tolerate only brief dips into his uncomfortable feelings. In his relationships he lost the confidence he relied on in his business. He became overly eager to please and responded with anxiety if his girlfriend was upset, even if her upset was unrelated to him.

I asked Mathew to describe the family he grew up in. Mathew said he's five years older than his younger brother, who has cerebral palsy. Theirs was a military family that moved every couple of years. Mathew had a protruding tooth, wore braces, and had thick glasses in elementary and middle school. On the playgrounds of two of the schools he attended, he was teased mercilessly. Mathew's parents were preoccupied with caring for his brother. Mathew was told repeatedly that he was the lucky one in the family. He never told his parents about the bullying. Long after his braces had been removed and his eyesight surgically corrected, Mathew carried within himself a sense of alienation and shame about being the ugly outsider who had no support.

After several sessions, Mathew described the upsetting evening with Gynene in detail. While they were cleaning up after dinner, Gynene had casually mentioned that she had gone for coffee that day with two co-workers, one, a woman from her office, and the other, Mike, an attractive man from a different department. Mathew (who had seen Mike from a distance once) had been shocked and dismayed. He felt betrayed. He pulled away from Gynene. She reacted first with disbelief, then attempted to reassure him that he, Mathew, was the person she wanted to be with and that she would have loved to have had him (Mathew) join them. She repeated that the coffee date was very casual and work-related and that she was "amazed" by his reaction. Mathew felt that she was pushing him aside and ignoring his feelings and was quietly outraged. He said he felt then that their relationship was "doomed." Because he so badly wanted things with Gynene to work out, he came for counselling.

I asked Mathew if he could feel the way he had felt the night of his distressing conversation with Gynene, even just a little. He said he could. I asked him to describe, as he talked to me, his feelings, and thoughts as they were that night. Mathew said, "I feel cold all over and I feel kind of sick to my stomach and I feel weak. I am telling myself nobody ever wants me." I asked Mathew if he had ever felt that way at an earlier time in his life. He said that the feelings felt familiar. I asked him if he felt any particular age as he talked. He looked surprised and said, "I felt this way a lot in school when I was around maybe eight, nine, or ten. When I went to a new school. When I had thick glasses, that damn tooth and braces and I got bullied all the time."

We carry with us, in our bodyminds, the various ages and stages of our lives during which we did or did not receive enough of the support, stimulation, or nurturing we needed to move successfully from one stage of our development to the next. We also hold in our bodies unintegrated shocks and trauma. When we're triggered in the present by a reminder of the painful past, the urgent demands of unmet needs can erupt and disrupt our lives. One way to talk about this is to speak as though we are talking about our inner child having needs.

Mathew now recognized the schoolyard origins of his strong reactive feelings toward Gynene when she told him she'd gone for coffee with a male co-worker. We talked briefly about how, because he knew his parents had been preoccupied and stressed by his brother's pressing needs, he'd wanted to protect them from more upset. Because of this, Mathew hadn't told them about his being bullied and they hadn't been there for him in a helpful way at that time. As a child, he'd endured bullying on his own. This was not to blame his parents, but to notice that he was affected by their absence.

In counselling, Mathew had learned and

had started to regularly practice the Breath Focusing-Tension Releasing techniques. He was learning to use Body Scanning to be alert to and release body tension before it cramped his shoulders. He was using the Friendship Filter and his Inner Coach to create a sense of inner safety. Using his non-judgmental Observer Self, he had learned to observe the flow of his feelings without making up elaborate self-defeating stories about himself. He was developing his emotional flexibility and was learning to trust himself. Because Mathew had learned to support himself in all these ways, I was comfortable asking him if he was interested in going a bit further in exploring and repairing his reactivity in his relationship. Mathew was eager to continue.

I suggested that he take three releasing and relaxing breaths. I let him know that this exercise required him to stay in his competent, confident adult self, the self who works, has his own place, goes on trips, and has adventures. Mathew said he believed he could do that. I then asked him if he had a sense or image of himself at eight, nine, or ten. "Oh yeah, sure," he said. "I'm the kid with braces standing as close as I can to the door, by myself." I asked Mathew to check in with himself; what were his feelings about that boy? He said, "I feel sorry for him, poor kid!" I asked Mathew if the boy was interested in talking with him. Mathew looked surprised, checked in with himself, and said the boy was "kind of curious." I then suggested that, in his imagination, adult Mathew approach the boy Mathew and let him know that he is who the boy grew up to be. I suggested to Mathew that he let the boy know that he is sorry he's having such a tough time and tell him (the boy-self) that he (grown-up Mathew) wants to visit him. Mathew agreed to this and nodded when I asked if the boy had agreed.

I then said to my client Mathew, "Ask the boy how he is feeling."

"Scared," came the answer.

"Ask him what else he is feeling," I instructed.

"Kind of hopeless."

"And one more time," I said, "What is he feeling?"

"Like nobody sees him or cares about him, and he's all alone," came the answer in a rush.

Mathew paused. "Kind of exactly like I was

feeling the night we argued." We sat in silence as Mathew digested his insight.

I then asked Mathew to bring his attention back into the room we were in by becoming very aware of his weight in the chair, of his feet on the floor, and to take some releasing, relaxing breaths. I asked him to reconnect with his resourceful adult self. Mathew did this.

Then it was time to go back to the boy.
"He told you he feels scared. Ask him what he needs," I said.
"Reassurance that he's going to be okay," said Mathew.
"He said he feels kind of hopeless. What does he need?" I asked a second time.
"Geez, I don't know," said Mathew.
"Give it a go," I encouraged him.
Mathew took a deep breath, puffed out an exhalation, and said, "Well, maybe to know that somebody's got his back. That kind of feels like it."
"One more time, ask him what he needs," I instructed.
"To know the kids like him, to know he's not alone, to know they get who he is," Mathew said.

I questioned, "To know that he is really safe and cared for, liked, and valued just as he is?"

"Exactly," came Mathew's answer.

The beauty of this exploration is that now grown-up triggered Mathew can offer himself what he needed and didn't get as a child. In doing this, he can deeply soothe himself in the present. As many people do, when he felt upset, vulnerable, and young, Mathew turned to the person closest to him, expecting her to help him feel better. It would serve Mathew and his relationship much more if he understands when he is triggered so that he can support his vulnerability with his own awareness and compassion. Once he feels calmer and more present, he can bring his concerns to his partner with interest and curiosity rather than making unwarranted assumptions that may escalate the couple's upset, potentially causing a rift and confusion in their relationship.

The next time Mathew feels triggered, uncertain, or jealous, as though he is unwanted in his relationship with Gynene, he knows he can turn to himself, take a moment to relax his body, and say to himself, "I know where these feelings come from. They are from when I was a lonely kid on the playground. That was then and this is now. I'm going to be okay. I was a super kid, I just didn't have support right then. Things are really different now. I've got friends and I know Gynene really cares for me."

Now when Mathew turns to Gynene, he will be up-to-date with himself and more available to what's happening in the present in his relationship, including his awareness of having been triggered.

EXERCISE 8.1 Time Travel Repair

Time Travel Repair is not a replacement for therapy. If, when you ask yourself how you feel about yourself as a child, you discover that you feel frightened or contemptuous or just wish the child would disappear, stop, and instead go to the short or rapid form of Time Travel Repair at the end of this chapter. Likewise, if you ask your child self if he or she wants to talk to you and the child turns away, hides, or is suspicious of you, do the same. Please respect yourself and the inner protections you've developed. They're there for good reasons. Don't bully yourself by pushing through any exercise that feels unsafe to you.

You'll need forty-five minutes of uninterrupted time for this exercise.

Make sure you have a glass of water or a cup of tea with you.

Start by gazing around at your surroundings paying particular attention to colors or any plants in the room.

Take three Breath Focusing-Tension Releasing breaths.

Feel your weight on the chair, the contact of your feet on the floor.

Review all three versions of Time Travel Repair before beginning this exercise.

Time Travel Repair, Long Form

Step 1: Feeling Triggered

- Think of a recent event during which you were triggered into old, unwanted, familiar feelings by the meaning you gave to that event.

At the time you may have felt quite righteous in your upset. You may have felt the need to protect yourself by lashing out or blaming. You may have felt defeated and retreated. You may have felt an inevitability about your reaction. Others may have pointed out that to them your response seemed out of proportion to what was happening at the time.

- Remind yourself, with compassion, that you were feeling triggered.

- Notice how you feel when you recall the triggering event. Do you have similar thoughts and feelings, perhaps less intense?

- Focus internally with an attitude of kind inquiry.

- Ask yourself, "How old do I feel?" If an age doesn't come, ask yourself, "When is the first time I remember feeling this way?" "What was happening around me then?"

- When you've identified your earlier age or circumstance, come back to the present. Turn away from the triggering thought, event, or person by anchoring on your breath. Say on your inhalation, silently, "Breathing in" and silently on your exhalation, "Breathing out." On your next inhalation, say silently to yourself, "Breathing in" and on your exhalation say, "Breathing out and letting go of tension. Softening. Coming into the present."

- Remind yourself of your current resourcefulness and how different your life is now compared to when you were much younger.

Step 2: Asking

- When you're feeling present, adult and resourced, go back

to the earlier time and ask yourself, "How do I feel about that young, vulnerable self? How does that younger self feel about me now"? If you have a sense that you are both okay to carry on, continue with the exercise. If you aren't sure, stop this exercise and go to Time Travel Repair, Short Form.

- If you've chosen to continue, tell your younger self that you are sorry she or he is having a hard time and ask: "What are you feeling?" Do this three times: "What are you feeling?"________________________X 3

- Each time, listen with soft, focused attention with your inner ear, sensing, and intuiting. The answer may come as a word, an emotion, or a felt sense. You might jot down the feelings so you can refer back to them. For example, your younger self might at first say, "ignored," the second time, "sad," and the third, "confused."

Come back to the present. Take three relaxing, releasing breaths. Feel your feet on the floor and your weight on the chair. Do a one full Body Scan Wave Breath and if you notice yourself holding tension, breathe into that area. Imagine tension releasing as you exhale. Soften your fingers and toes.

Step 3: Important Questions

- Now, go back to your younger self in your fully resourced adult state.

- Ask your younger self what he or she needs given how he or she is feeling. Ask three times, once for each feeling: "What do you need?"___________________________X 3

- Make mental or written notes on the answers you get. If the first feeling was 'ignored', your younger self might want to feel acknowledged and included. The sad younger self might want to feel cared for and appreciated, while the confused younger self might want some clear explanation or direction from a trusted adult.

Once you've done this refocus on your surroundings. Gaze around the room. Feel your weight in the chair. Your feet on the ground. Take several full breaths. Stand up and stretch. Have some water if you are thirsty.

Step 4: Comfort and Parent

- Use these answers about what was needed by you back then, and that you didn't get, to comfort and compassionately parent yourself with your Inner Ideal Parent when you feel triggered into those younger, vulnerable feelings in the present.

- Imagine that you are sending your words to both your younger and your present selves. In doing this, you can deeply soothe yourself in the present.

- Remember to use a BFTR technique to let go of tension.

To summarize, if in the present you are feeling young, ignored, sad, and confused you can turn to yourself with all your adult awareness and parent yourself with compassion saying something like, "I've been time traveling; these feelings are from long ago. Things are different now. I now know how to care for myself and acknowledge myself. I appreciate myself in many ways." Remind yourself that although you felt ignored, sad, and confused back then, now you have many more resources and ways to make sense of the earlier situation as well as ways to make sense of what's happening in your life now. Remind yourself of ways you are included, acknowledged, appreciated, and cared for in your current life, both by yourself and by others.

Take a moment or two to settle into the experience of Time Travel Repair that you have just offered yourself. Use your Observer Self to notice how you feel in your bodymind.

Come into the present now feeling adult, resourceful, calm, and confident.

Jot a few notes about this experience for future reference.

In the Time Travel Repair Long Form exercise, you use combinations of the Breath Focusing-Tension Releasing technique, the Observer Self, your Ideal Inner Parent, and Body Scanning.

Time Travel Repair, Short Form

When you are aware of feeling triggered, do the following:

Step 1: Anchor and Coach

- Anchor on your breath.

- Say to yourself: "These are old, familiar feelings from a long time ago. No need to revisit the past. That was then and this is now. In the present I am resourceful and safe enough. I'm going to be okay. I accept myself as I am. What is, is. My job is to calm myself."

Step 2: Release Tension, Come Present

- Take three Focusing-Tension Releasing breaths.

- Shift your focus. Come present.

Step 3: Acknowledge Yourself

- Acknowledge yourself for having the ability to make conscious life-affirming choices.

Time Travel Repair, Even Shorter Version

If the Time Travel Short Form words don't fit you, here is a useful and even shorter version of Time Travel Repair:

Step 1: Anchor and Acknowledge

- Breathe in. Anchor on your breath.

- Acknowledge your reactivity. Say to yourself, "Right now, I am feeling tense and triggered."

Step 2: Drop and Coach

- Exhale. Drop the trigger—let it go as though it is a hot potato. Soften your fingers and toes as you do this.

- Coach yourself: "Letting go. That was then; this is now."

Step 3: Come Present and Acknowledge

- Shift your focus. Come present

- Acknowledge yourself for having made conscious, life-affirming choices.

- Shift your focus. Come into the present. Continue to use relaxing breaths.

Now that you can recognize when you are triggered and know how to use Time Travel Repair effectively, you can choose to be more present in your relationships with yourself, your friends, partners, family, and workmates.

(Adapted from Calling in The One Coach Training, Katherine Woodward Thomas, M.A., MFT, 2011, used with permission).

Having worked through the exercises in *One Choice at a Time*, you now know how to untangle the tired old web of limiting beliefs that said you were "too much" or "not enough" of something. You can support and celebrate yourself. You know how to be self-respectful; how to make choices based on your values; how to acknowledge your worth and lovability; how to care for your marvelous body.

Don't be surprised if you find yourself with more clarity, confidence, and creativity in every aspect of your life.

CHAPTER 9: WHAT MATTERS MOST

"My barn having burned to the ground, I can now see the moon." ~*Masahide*

The tearful man sitting in my office appeared shrunken and closed in on himself. He seemed embarrassed but was determined to speak. He was in his early seventies.

Edgar's Story

"Nothing makes sense to me anymore." he was saying. "I worked hard my entire life, raised my family. My wife died two years ago; my kids are gone. My life has no meaning. I don't know why I should bother anymore." Edgar was feeling isolated, useless, and anxious. He had told his doctor that he wasn't sure he wanted to live

anymore. This had frightened them both and Edgar's doctor, whom I had met when I worked as a nurse in psychiatry, had arranged for this visit.

Edgar was having an existential crisis.

Often people open up to questions about what gives their lives a sense of purpose and meaning at times of transition or crisis—when they are stretched or shaken out of their familiar ways of coping.

I told Edgar that I thought he was touching on some of the essential questions that most human beings grapple with at some point in their lives. Edgar's relief was palpable hearing that he had company in his concerns. I asked him if there had been times in his life when he'd felt that things made sense to him and that his life did have meaning. He said he'd always been busy, "doing what needed to be done", and hadn't ever thought about such things. I asked him if he was willing to take this time to look at his life in ways he may have never done before. As we talked, I encouraged him to remember times in his life when he had felt useful and had enjoyed himself, to find possible clues about what made him feel that his life had purpose.

It turned out that Edgar had relied on his wife to provide him with contact and a sense of connection. He was crushingly lonely. As we talked, Edgar decided he had primarily derived his sense of meaning and purpose in providing for and serving his family. He desperately wanted to feel useful. In that first conversation, Edgar began to make sense of the inner desolation he was feeling and started to recognize the essential humanity in the questions he was posing. Edgar's pain, his relief at being heard, and his eagerness to make sense of his experience touched me deeply.

We would go on to explore ways in which he could reconnect with what most mattered to him. For example, by expanding his sense of family to include people in his larger community, and by finding out where there might be needs he could fill, Edgar could choose to provide valuable service, thus supporting his own desire to contribute.

At any age or stage of life, we need to realign with what provides us meaning and purpose when we are jarred—or drift—off course.

EXERCISE 9.1 Review and More Questions

Choose a time when you have an uninterrupted hour.

Have your pen and paper or computer handy.

Have a glass of water or your favorite beverage close by.

Take a moment to feel your weight on the chair and your feet on the floor. Settle in.

As you answer the questions in this chapter, write freely, with no censoring. As with previous exercises, your writing is for your eyes only unless you choose to share it.

Take three focused, relaxing breaths.

Step 1: Review

In *Chapter 1: Beneficial Attitudes*, you learned to adopt attitudes that will be helpful for you as you learn new self-supporting skills, navigate life's challenges and embark on any life journey.

These attitudes are kindness, willingness, interest and curiosity, trust, patience, self-responsibility, and necessary self-care.

I'm going to add two more beneficial attitudes here that will support you in your efforts to maintain the skills you have learned. The first is the attitude of **determination**—unwavering resolve to return to practices and routines that you know are beneficial for you because you feel so much better when you do them. The second is the attitude of **persistence**—carrying on in the face of inevitable challenges and difficulties. With determination and persistence, you'll be unstoppable!

- Of the beneficial attitudes suggested here, which has been the most challenging for you to adopt? Why do you think that is?

- Which feels the most natural to you? Why do you think this is?

- Are there other beneficial attitudes that you have or want to develop that will support you to maintain your peace of mind and overall well-being?

In *Chapter 2: Relaxed Anticipation,* you learned the Breath Focusing-Tension Releasing techniques and **Box Breathing**. Mastered and integrated, these powerful practices can support you through everyday challenges as well as times of crisis. You were introduced to the practice of taking tension-managing **Mini-Breaks** to bring more relaxation and pleasure into your life.

- What was the first thing you noticed shifting when you started to build in breath-focusing relaxation practices during times of minor irritations?

- Which of these practices do you find most accessible and practical when you are faced with a tough situation?

- What, if anything, gets in the way of your taking mini-relaxation breaks? If you forget to do them, what can you build into your daily routines to remind yourself to shift and take a mini-break?

In *Chapter 3: Your Living Goals,* you updated your goals and explored why they're important to you. You learned how to use your **Living Goals** to keep yourself on track when making decisions. You saw how your outdated **Old Guard** beliefs have worked to hold you back from achieving what you've wanted. You learned how to acknowledge them compassionately, and challenge and transform those old beliefs.

- Do your goals continue to support you in moving toward what matters most to you?

- Are you embodying and living your values? How do you feel about that?

- How do you respond when outdated, undermining beliefs surface?

You created your **Resource Inventory** in *Chapter 4: Lightening Up,* to remind yourself of your resources, gifts, and many blessings, and to refer to when you feel self-critical and "less than." You created a **Resource Reminder**, a description of yourself flourishing and on track, to energize and encourage yourself. The wonderful, healing **Gratitude Practice** was introduced.

- What do you find most helpful about reviewing your Resource Inventory?'

- Do you notice your posture or breathing change when you say your Resource Reminder sentence or sentences?

- What is the best thing about your Gratitude Practice?

In *Chapter 5: Take Your Best Friend with You*, **the Open Door, Closed Door Exercise** was used to illustrate the powerful impact of your own words on your well-being. You learned to develop a respectful and kind relationship with yourself using the **Friendship Filter** questions. You developed your **Inner Coach** and **Ideal Inner Parent** as supportive voices.

- What have you noticed shifting in your relationships at home and at work as you create a kinder, more accepting inner life for yourself?

- What has been your main challenge in developing your ideal inner parents?

In *Chapter 6: Fascinating Stories*, you learned the benefit of developing an accepting, non-reactive, kind **Observer Self**.

Over time this focusing practice will help you create the inner spaciousness you need to give yourself choice in how you respond to both inner events—such as outdated storytelling—and outer events.

- What has been the most beneficial outcome for you in developing your Observer Self?

- What was most difficult for you in this chapter? Do you know why this was?

- Are you able to stay non-judgmental when you notice what is difficult for you? What's that like for you?

In *Chapter 7: Supporting the Wisdom Body*, you were given a set of **Body Wake-Up Exercises** to use to start your day feeling alert and relaxed. You were led through a **Full Body Relaxation**, an excellent end-of-day practice. **Body Scanning** was introduced as a way to check in and release tension from tight muscles during your busy day. A technique for **Embodying with Breath** was described.

- Did you adapt the Body Wake-Up, Full Body Relaxation, Body Scanning, and Embodying with Breath exercises to your unique abilities?

- After several weeks of regularly doing the Body Wake-Up exercises and incorporating Body Scanning, what has shifted in the way you carry yourself physically?

In *Chapter 8: Time Traveling*, the powerful **Time Travel Exercises** were introduced. Either the **Long or Short Forms of Time Travel Repair** can be useful if you are reactive in your current relationships.

- How has the concept of Time Travel shifted your understanding of what you bring to your relationships?

- Now that you are more aware of the vulnerability that underlies defensiveness and reactivity, have you noticed yourself feeling more compassionate toward yourself (and others) when you (or they) are lost in a reactive moment? Can you elaborate on this?

Chapter 9: What Matters Most, started with **questions of meaning and purpose**, I've reviewed the content of each chapter and offered some questions for each.

Step 2: More Questions

Like Edgar, as you move through different life stages, you may find yourself having to define or redefine what gives your life meaning and purpose.

The following are questions designed to facilitate your exploration of that important topic. Go gently with yourself and remember to bring non-judgmental kindness and curiosity to your inquiries. Allow yourself to hold the questions lightly and with inner spaciousness. You could imagine that you are dropping the questions into a deep pond and waves will ripple out and come back, perhaps with even more questions. Practice living with not knowing. Let the questions ripen.

You may want to sit quietly with your journal and write whatever comes, stream-of-consciousness style, or you may find that your answers come at surprising times, seemingly out of the blue. There is no right or wrong.

One person may derive meaning in gardening and giving away surplus fruits and vegetables to food banks; for another, tracing and documenting family history may provide a sense of purpose. Yet another may say, "I'm on point with myself when I am in the present with an open heart."

- **What are your clues that you are on or off track with yourself?**

- **What makes your life meaningful?**

- **Do you get to decide what your life purpose is?**

- **Do your goals support you to live your purpose in the present?**

- **If you have spiritual beliefs, do you use them to guide and support yourself in your daily life?**

- **What expands your perspective and lifts you beyond your self-imposed limitations?**

- What helps you feel connected—to yourself, to the people and creatures you know, to the natural world, to your larger human community?

- When you want to explore the bigger questions in your life, where can you turn for guidance, support, or inspiration?

My own answers to these questions continue to shift and change over time. Once I would have said that learning was what provided my life with meaning, at another time, sensory experience, and at another, a moment of service or connection.

Creating Your Daily Morning Practices

You may already have daily practices that nourish and inspire you. If you don't have such practices, now is the time to start.

It doesn't have to be complicated. For example, it may be taking ten to fifteen minutes for meditation or prayer; your gratitude practice; then reading an inspiring passage; some study; or watching an uplifting video before you launch into your day. It might be a walk in nature. Or listening to uplifting music.

Whatever your Morning Practices, intend to be fully present for them and use that time to remind yourself of what is most important to you. Let that provide the foundation for

your day—that and a morning Body Wake-up Practice and an exercise routine!

- Think of practices or rituals you'll incorporate into your morning routine that will inspire you and provide you with a sense of meaningful connection with what matters to you.

- Check-in with yourself throughout your day to see if you are still in touch with your uplifted morning practice feelings. If you aren't, take time to remember and feel what matters to you and inspires you before you carry on.

If this is new to you, experiment with starting your day with daily practices for at least several months to experience the benefits of integrating them fully into your life.

Whatever goals you set for yourself in Chapter 3, in practicing and integrating the skills you've learned in *ONE CHOICE AT A TIME: A Practical Guide to Peace of Mind and Well-Being*, you've had the opportunity to become a more peaceful, kinder, more compassionate, confident, and resilient human being. Through repeated practice, you're learning to trust yourself and to access your own values-based inner knowing for moment-to-moment guidance as you make your decisions. You've learned lifetime practices that can support your peace of mind, your vitality, spontaneity, overall well-being, and flourishing—even in the

face of uncertainty and unprecedented challenges. **You can do this.**

One conscious breath at a time, one life-affirming choice at a time.

Dear Reader,

I'm grateful that you've shared some of your precious time with me. I'd love to know what difference reading and engaging with this book has made to the quality of your life. You can connect with me at susan@susanfarling.com. Thank you.

Warmly,

Susan

Exercise Inventory

1.1 Experience a Closed Attitude versus a Willing Attitude: Use this simple exercise to experience how your physical posture impacts your inner state.

2.1 Breath Focusing-Tension Releasing Techniques: Learn to release bodymind tension in the face of everyday irritations and challenging situations. Support your peace of mind, clarity, and confidence when you are able to calmly and thoughtfully respond rather than react in old unhelpful ways.

2.2 Box Breathing: A powerful breath exercise used by Navy Seals given here to offer you a choice of techniques.

2.3 Mini-Breaks: Build refreshing mini-breaks into your busy life to support your relaxation, enjoyment and vitality.

3.1 Clarifying and Aligning Your Goals and Values: Develop confidence and clarity in your values-based decision-making. Live with purpose and meaning.

3.2 Old Guard Objections: Compassionately understand, recognize, and release your inner resistance to developing new desirable habits.

4.1 Resource Inventory: Increase your confidence and trust in your resilience and resourcefulness. Fully acknowledge your talents, self-supportive qualities, supports and connections.

4.2 Resource Reminder: Create a powerful statement that will help you embody your most resourced self.

4.3 Attitude of Gratitude: Nourish your overall well-being with a regular embodied gratitude practice.

5.1 Friendship Filter: Use this powerful three-question filter to develop, support and maintain your inner kindness, self-respect, and confidence.

5.2 Inner Coach: Use self-coaching to support and encourage yourself through challenging situations.

5.3 Inner Ideal Parent: Take over the role of a loving internal parent or caregiver.

6.1 Observer Self: Offer yourself a path to peace of mind, and the ability to be more present and non-reactive in your daily life.

7.1 Body Wake-Up Exercises: Support your vitality and flexibility with this simple, gentle series of exercises.

7.2 Full-Body Relaxation: Lower your level of overall tension by regular use of this full-body relaxation.

7.3 Body Scanning: Use this series of techniques to regularly check-in with the wealth of information provided by your physical sensations, thoughts, emotions, and feelings. Be aware of your level of tension and intervene with tension releasing techniques.

7.4 Embodying Preferred States: Support development of your preferred inner qualities through visualization and breath.

8.1 Time Travel Repair: Learn to recognize when you are reacting to your past rather than to the present in your current relationships. Use this information to compassionately bring yourself up-to-date and be more present with yourself and the people around you.

9.1 Review and More Questions: Review of each chapter and questions to help you consolidate what has been useful for you in going through the exercises in this book. Focusing questions regarding creating a meaningful and inspired life.

REFERENCES, INFLUENCES AND RESOURCES

Benson, H. *The Relaxation Response.* New York, NY: William Morrow, 1975.

Borysenko, Joan. *Minding the Body, Mending the Mind.* New York, NY: Bantam, 1988.

Borysenko, Joan. *Guilt is the Teacher, Love is the Lesson.* New York, NY: Warner, 1990.

Braden, Gregg. *Secrets of the Lost Mode of Prayer: The Hidden Power of Beauty, Blessing, Wisdom and Hurt.* Carlsbad, CA: Hay House, 2006.

Brown, Michael. *The Presence Process: A Healing Journey into Present Moment Awareness.* Vancouver, Canada: Namaste, 2005.

Carrington, Patricia. *Discover the Power of Meridian Tapping: A Revolutionary Method for Stress-Free Living.* Brookfield, CT: The Tapping Solution, 2008.

Chabris, Christopher & Simons, Daniel. *The Invisible Gorilla Test: On the Phenomenon of Inattention Blindness*. Research paper. Cambridge, MA: Harvard University, 2004.

Chödrön, Pema. *When Things Fall Apart: Heart Advice for Difficult Times*. Boulder, CO: Shambhala, 1997.

Chopra, Deepak, M.D. and Tanzi, Rudolph E., Ph.D. *Super Brain: Unleashing the Explosive Power of Your Mind to Maximize Health, Happiness, and Spiritual Well-Being*. New York, NY: Harmony, 2012.

Dispenza, Joe. *Becoming Supernatural: How Common People Are Doing the Uncommon*. Carlsbad, CA: Hay House, 2017.

Dispenza, Joe. *Breaking the Habit of Being Yourself: How to Lose Your Mind and Create a New One*. Carlsbad, CA: Hay House, 2013.

Dispenza, Joe. *You Are the Placebo: Making Your Mind Matter*. Carlsbad, CA: Hay House, 2014.

Dwoskin, Hale. *The Sedona Method: Your Key to Lasting Happiness, Success, Peace and Emotional Well-Being*. Minnetonka, MN: Sedona, 2007.

Dychtwald, K. *Body-Mind*. New York, NY: Jove, 1977.

Emoto, Masaru. *The Hidden Messages in Water*. Hillsboro, OR: Beyond Words, 2004.

Ferrucci, Piero. *The Power of Kindness: The Unexpected Benefits of Leading a Compassionate Life*. New York, NY: Penguin, 2007.

Frankl, Victor. *Man's Search for Meaning*. Boston, MA: Beacon, 1959.

Gawain, Shakti. *Creative Visualization: Use the Power of Your Imagination to Create What You Want in Your Life*. Novato, CA: New World Library, 1978.

Gendlin, E.T. *Focusing (2nd ed.)*. New York, NY: Bantam, 1978.

Goleman, Daniel. *Emotional Intelligence*. New York, NY: Bantam, 1995.

Hanh, Thich Nhat. *Essential Writings*. New York, NY: Orbis, 2001.

Hanson, Rick & Mendius, Richard. *The Practical Neuroscience of Buddha's Brain: Happiness, Love & Wisdom*. Oakland, CA: New Harbinger, 2009.

Hawkins, David. *Letting Go: The Pathway of Surrender*. Carlesbad, CA: Hay House, 2012.

Huffington, Arianna. *The Sleep Revolution: Transforming Your Life One Night At A Time*. New York, NY: Harmony, 2016.

Huseyin, Naci & Ioannidis, John. *Evaluation of Wellness Determinants and Interventions by Citizen Scientists*. (Jul 14;314(2):121-2), JAMA, 2015.

Kabat-Zinn, Jon. *Full Catastrophe Living: Using the Wisdom of Your Body and Mind to Face Stress, Pain, and Illness.* New York, NY: Bantam Doubleday Dell, 1990.

Kabat-Zinn, Jon and Williams, Mark G. (editors). *Mindfulness: Diverse Perspectives on its Meaning, Origins and Applications.* New York, NY: Routledge, 2013.

Katie, Byron. *The Work.* www.thework.com

Kersey, Cynthia. *Unstoppable: 45 Powerful Stories of Perseverance and Triumph from People Just Like You.* Naperville, IL: Source Books, 1998.

Khan, Sufi Inayat. *The Book of Health.* London, UK: Sufi, 1974.

Krishnamurti, Jiddu. *Think on These Things.* New York, NY: Harper & Row, 1964.

Kurtz, R. & Prestera, H. *The Body Reveals: An Illustrated Guide to the Psychology of the Body.* New York, NY: Harper & Row, 1976.

Lau, D.C. (transl.) *Lao Tzu: Tao Te Ching.* London, UK: Penguin, 1963.

Levine, Peter. *Waking the Tiger: Healing Trauma.* Berkeley, CA: North Atlantic, 1997.

Levine, Stephen. *Healing into Life and Death.* New York: Anchor, 1989.

Lipton, Bruce. *The Biology of Belief: Unleashing the Power of Consciousness, Matter & Miracles.* Carlsbad, CA: Hay House, 2008.

MacNaughton, Ian (editor). *Body, Breath, & Consciousness: A Somatics Anthology. A Collection of Articles on Family Systems, Self-Psychology, The Bodynamics Model of Somatic Developmental Psychology, Shock Trauma, and Breathwork.* Berkeley, CA: North Atlantic, 2004.

McTaggart, Lynne. *The Intention Experiment: Using Your Thoughts to Change Your Life and the World.* New York, NY: Simon & Schuster, 2007.

Miller, Dr. Richard C. *The iRest Program for Healing PTSD: A Proven-Effective Approach to Using Yoga Nidra Meditation & Deep Relaxation Techniques to Overcome Trauma.* Oakland, CA: New Harbinger, 2015.

Myss, Caroline. *Why People Don't Heal and How They Can.* New York, NY: Three Rivers, 1997.

Nyhan, B. & Reifler J. *When Corrections Fail. The Persistence of Political Misperceptions.* Political Behavior, (32(2), 303–3302010), 2010.

Ortner, Nick. *The Tapping Solution: A Revolutionary System for Stress-Free Living.* Carlsbad, CA: Hay House. 2014.

Pert, Candace. *Molecules of Emotion: The Science Behind Mind-Body Medicine*. New York, NY: Touchstone, 1999.

Rydall, Derek. *Emergence: Seven Steps for Radical Life Change*. New York, NY: Simon & Schuster, 2015.

Salzberg, Sharon. *Loving-Kindness: The Revolutionary Art of Happiness*. Boulder, CA: Shambhala, 1995.

Seigel, M.D., Bernie. *Love, Medicine and Miracles. Lessons Learned about Self-Healing from a Surgeon's Experience with Exceptional Patients*. New York, NY: Harper & Row, 1986.

Siegel, Daniel. J. *Mindsight: The New Science of Personal Transformation*. New York, NY: Bantam, 2011.

Siegel, Daniel J. *The Mindful Brain: Reflection and Attunement in the Cultivation of Well-Being. New York, NY:* Norton, 2007.

Sivananda, Swami. *Thought-Power: The Right Methods of Handling and Manipulating Thought for the Best Benefit of Man*. Rishikesh, India: The Divine Life Society, 1980.

Sprinkling (Farling), Susan. *Hatha Yoga and Counselling: A Phenomenological Investigation*. M.A. Thesis. Victoria, BC: University of Victoria, 1986.

Suzuki, Shunryu. *Zen Mind, Beginner's Mind*. New York, NY: Weatherhill, 1970.

Suzuki, Shunryu. *Zen Mind Beginner's Mind Transcripts, Lecture on Posture*. Los Altos, CA, 1965.

Tulku, Tarthang. *Gesture of Balance: A Guide to Awareness, Self-Healing, and Meditation*. Cazadero, CA: Dharma Publishing, 1977.

Wilber, Ken. *The Spectrum on Consciousness*. Wheaton, IL: Quest Books, 1977.

Wilber, Ken. *The Atman Project: A Transpersonal View of Human Development*. Wheaton, IL: Quest Books, 1980.

Wilber, Ken. *Grace and Grit: Spirituality and Healing in the Life and Death of Treya Kilam Wilber*. Boulder, CA: Shambhala, 1991.

Wilber, Ken. *Integral Spirituality: A Startling New Role for Religion in the Modern and Postmodern World*. Boston, MA: Integral Books, 2006.

ACKNOWLEDGEMENTS

It's the stories of people, facing their challenges, determined to make positive changes in their lives, that bring *ONE CHOICE AT A TIME* alive. As a nurse, counsellor, psychotherapist, and coach I've been profoundly touched and inspired to be present for and help facilitate my client's journeys to what truly matters most to them.

Thanks and appreciation to my family, friends, and colleagues who have remained encouraging of this project through the delays and ups and downs of my learning curves.

Alysha, your counsel, steadfast faith in my abilities, and inspiring example of a woman going flat out for her dreams have helped me stay steady on course.

Thanks to Somatic Trauma Work Psychotherapist and now retired U Vic Assistant Teaching Professor, Yvonne Haist and to Retired Clinical Psychologist Dr. Gary Deatherage for their helpful critiques that contributed to the robust structure of the book and to the clarity of the ideas expressed in the first edition.

Thanks again to Margaret Hantiuk for her proofreading and editing skills in the first edition. Margaret helped me recognize and let go of jargon and thus get closer to my goal of having this be a straightforward and easily accessible book.

Finally, my ongoing appreciation goes to Dan Doherty of Reciprocity Publishing for his continued support of this project and for his encouragement of the birth of Germaine Publishing.

About the Author

Susan Farling's working life started in her teens and twenties with a rich and instructive hodgepodge of jobs (in a mill, laundry, bank, factory, hospital, daycare centre, arts co-operative, community art centre, entomology lab). Her formal education took her from an undergraduate arts degree to training as a registered nurse and working in acute care psychiatry and mental health for a decade. In her late thirties, she obtained a master's degree in counselling psychology and was a founding member of a thriving counselling center where she enjoyed a thirty-year counselling and psychotherapy general private practice. Currently, her focus has expanded to include coaching with an emphasis on second and third stage of life transitions such as retirement, ageing, and the impact of ageism.

Susan is a besotted mother and grandmother and a lover of trees, poetry, and good stories. She is everlastingly grateful for her family and friends, especially for the Full Circle Community, the Sovereign Sisters Power Pod, and the CUPS camping buddies.

Connect with Susan at www.susanfarling.com

Your review of *ONE CHOICE AT A TIME: A Practical Guide to Peace of Mind and Well-Being* would be very helpful for potential readers and greatly appreciated by me. Thanks!

For your free

ONE CHOICE AT A TIME

Full Body Relaxation Audio go to

susanfarling.com/free-gift-audio-full-body-relaxation-lp/

NOTES